Get Visible And Attract
Clients To Your Business

Tom Adams

Flourish Press, Inc.

Copyright © 2012 by Tom Adams. All rights reserved under all copyright conventions. No part of this book shall be reproduced, stored in a retrieval system, or transmitted by any means, electronic, mechanical, photocopying, recording, or otherwise, without written permission from the publisher.

Disclaimer: This book and the information contained herein are for informative purposes only. The information in this book is distributed on an "As Is" basis, without warranty. The author makes no legal claims, express or implied, and the material is not meant to substitute legal or financial counsel. The author, publisher and/or copyright holder assume no responsibility for the loss or damage caused, or allegedly caused, directly or indirectly by the use of the information in this book. Throughout the book trademarked names are referenced. Rather than putting a trademark symbol in every occurrence of the trademarked name, we state that we are using the names in an editorial fashion only and to the benefit of the trademark owner with no intention of infringement upon the trademark. The fact that a person or organization is referred to as a citation and/or a potential source of information does not mean that the author or the publisher endorses them.

Published by Flourish Press, Inc.
3525 Del Mar Heights Road, Suite 383
San Diego, CA 92130 USA
Telephone: 800-450-5390   Web: FlourishPress.com
For special orders or bulk purchases, please contact Flourish Press.

Publisher's Cataloging-in-Publication data

Adams, Tom Alan.
    You are the logo: get visible and attract clients to your business / Tom Adams.
    p. cm.
    ISBN 978-0-9849920-0-3
 1. Branding (Marketing). 2. Small business marketing. 3. Marketing. 4. Advertising. 5. Small business – Management. 6. Self-presentation. 7. Success in business. 8. Internet marketing. I. Title.

HF5415 .A52 2012
658.8--dc23   2012933604

Cover Illustration by Nicholas Samuel Adams
Book Design and Layout by Melissa Puleo Adams
Editing by Sheryl Roush
First Edition
Printed in United States of America

For Sawyer, Knox and Emma

Acknowledgements

To Bob Johnson who serendipitously provided the hard deadline for me to finish this book.

To Mike Sullivan for always being willing to learn and test these ideas out in his life and business.

To Dan Kennedy who has been an incredible marketing mentor to me over the last eight years.

To the incredible staff at Flourish Press: Melissa Adams for her persistent management of deadlines as well as the layout, design and production of this book; Nick Adams for the cover design work; Sawyer Adams for his stable presence; and the rest of the team – for their dedicated support and care of our clients.

To Sheryl Roush for her exceptional editorial and advisory guidance. This book is infinitely better because of her.

To David Young for his proofreading prowess and catching those previously overlooked items.

To all the incredible people who have served as guides, educators, advisors and examples to me over the years. Without them there would have been nothing to write.

Finally, this book would not have been possible without the input, effort, and support given it by Becky Adams – my wife, best friend and business partner. Her understanding, patience and love make me the luckiest man in the world.

Forward

The creation of a business logo is not an easy thing. It is often an intense and difficult discovery process. It starts with a concept, a name, and a dream to create something artistic to succinctly tie these all together.

Then, it is placed into the skillful hands of a trusted designer to craft it in such a way that it represents all that business is about. It should be fresh and modern. It should capture the style and flavor of the personality of the company. It should be original yet not crazy or ridiculous.

As the owner of a marketing company that has produced a significant amount of corporate logos over the years, this can be a terrifying process from a designer's perspective. After studying a client and their business, a designer begins the task of creating a number of different ideas that represent what the company wants. These concepts are refined and adjusted creating a number of options to show the client. Occasionally, designers might include a design or two that are inherently risky, but still need to be shown.

This is where the fun begins and when the client starts to interact with the design options.

Design is incredibly subjective. A logo treatment that feels comfortable and is less risky might edge out what might be a less comfortable, bold new design. There is a considerable amount of time invested with design options including the choice of colors and artistic nuances. Thus, the process goes back and forth from client to designer. This can drag on for weeks (if not months) with a single decision maker. If a committee is involved, as it often is, then the path to a completed piece of logo art is even more complicated.

When the final decision is made and the final logo is chosen, it's promptly affixed to all manner of identity pieces, from business cards to websites, letterhead, signage, and more.

It is at this point that there is a feeling of success and accomplishment in the mind of the business owner or executive. The critical and important brand building activity is finalized. For many new companies it is the mark of being "professional" or "having arrived." For some, it is the renewal or evolution of a corporate image.

For others, it is the beginning of a glimmer of hope that this small piece of artistic design will become the icon that draws people to them. It is also the dream that this icon will be the representation of the company in its fullest form.

Unfortunately, the effort extended to create a simple, inanimate representation of your business is given much more strategic attention than the one thing that holds a significantly higher value.

This one thing has a much greater capacity to impact the success of the business and organization. It will help prospects determine if your business is worthy of their choice. In fact, it may be the ultimate positioning device. This icon could shape the entire destiny of your company.

The icon I refer to is you.

You Are The Logo!

Table of Contents

Forward	ix
Introduction	1

Section 1: Foundations

1	Does It Work?	7
2	A Better Way	17
3	The Time Is Now	25
4	Some Marketing Refreshers	35
5	The "You" Required	43
6	Craft Your Positioning	53
7	You Are The Logo Design	63

Section 2: How To Implement

8	A Logo Speaks	81
9	A Logo Writes	89
10	A Logo Writes Repeatedly	97
11	A Logo Advertises	105
12	A Logo Publicizes	113
13	A Logo Associates	121
14	A Logo Publishes	129
15	A Logo Engages	135

Conclusion	141
Afterward	143
You Are The Logo™ Support Services	145
About The Author	147

Introduction

It has been said that we do not see the world as it is, but as we are. As a result, my perspective on the power of iconic, personality-based marketing is rooted in my own unique story.

I am a passionate, life-long student of marketing as well as a consultant who has been paid to advise and coach numerous companies, business owners and executives about their own marketing. I have had the opportunity to study and observe what works and what doesn't.

I have also observed and studied hundreds of other companies which have shown me the proven power of this alternative approach to marketing.

Even more importantly, I have used my own life and business as the ultimate experiment and proving ground for my unique style of marketing.

My foundations for a "You Are The Logo" way of marketing were shaped from my earliest memories. These ideas did not come from a business perspective, but from a church and ministry context. Dad and Grandpa were both preachers. Early in my life they were preachers that did not have a home parish or church; they were "circuit preachers." They toured from church to church having been invited to minister to that particular congregation.

Their income and livelihood was, to a great extent, dependent on establishing the type of trust and reputation that attracted repeat invitations from these congregations. So from an early time in my life, my earliest role models for marketing (Dad, Grandpa and their peers) were always working at something that created for them an established level of trust, likeability, credibility and attractiveness as an individual.

Being the eldest son, I followed in their footsteps and became a minister, though only in a single congregation. I realized very quickly, that the relative success of a church is greatly determined by the effectiveness, charisma and capability of the minister leading that congregation.

While I did not remain in the profession for long, the things I learned about personality-based leadership in that setting have had a significant impact on my subsequent entrepreneurial and business ventures.

My story winds its way through the clothing industry where I co-founded and managed a small, regional chain of retail menswear stores. (It's more a story of defeat than victory, but the lessons from it were profound!)

I spent almost ten years as a corporate trainer, motivational speaker and management consultant which allowed me to meet and teach thousands of people from every walk of life, as well as to sit at boardroom tables with C-Level executives. Within this role, my experiences are too numerous to mention, but a memorable one included working with an Aborigine Medical Center in the Outback of Australia. I have worked with government agencies, private enterprise, Fortune 500 companies and everything else in between.

It was during this period of my life that I also produced and hosted two separate television series. This led to even more interesting learning experiences in the broadcast world, one of which included co-hosting a daytime TV talk show.

For a few of years after that, I had the privilege to partner with my brother, Stan Adams, in his business. I became deeply involved in the commercial records management industry during this phase of my business life. As is always the case, everything you learn along the way keeps setting you up for where you will go next.

In 2003, I formed Flourish Press with a passionate belief that the primary goal of my life, and as a result, my business, would be to help people and their businesses flourish and thrive. And in these last nine years, I have marketed the services of the business using the framework, the mindset and the strategies I will outline in this book.

I will share stories showing what I have learned along the way. In addition, I will share the stories of those with whom I have worked and advised. Their stories confirm the effectiveness of my personality-based style of marketing. There are also numerous business personalities that I will point out as examples of You Are The Logo style marketing.

In reading this book, my hope is that you will learn my method of marketing. It is an alternative to the more generic, "brand-based" marketing approach that we commonly see in the marketplace.

This is not to say that brand-based marketing is wrong for all businesses. However, a traditional brand-based approach to marketing makes it difficult to distinguish what makes one company different from another.

While I originally wrote this book for owners, entrepreneurs, executives and professionals mostly in service-focused businesses, it is also very helpful to anyone who wants to enhance their current career or start a new one simply by applying my principles.

You will be provided with a solid foundation to recognize the kind of personality that is required in this type of marketing. In addition, I will give you an overview of the kind of activities, tactics and marketing tools you need to make it happen.

Finally, I must remind you that this is not an instant success formula. It is a marketing approach. It's my strategy that will make you more visible to your prospect marketplace. You will evolve as you become more comfortable in your new marketing role. This is a journey, a process and an evolution.

As the Logo for my own business, I have found it to be an incredible journey. I invite you to join me.

Tom Adams

SECTION 1

Foundations of You Are The Logo Marketing

Nobody can prevent you from choosing to be exceptional.
Mark Sanborn

CHAPTER 1

Does It Work?

*Few things are harder to put up with than the
annoyance of a good example.*
Mark Twain

To compete effectively in today's business world as a business owner, executive, professional or entrepreneur, you must be the marketing icon and personality spokesperson for your business. You must be visible and overt. You must be the Logo.

To illustrate this, I share a few examples of well-known business people that have chosen this specific marketing strategy to help grow their business.

The Donald

Donald Trump exemplifies the essence of a company built and developed based on leveraging himself as the iconic spokesperson and Logo for his Trump businesses and licenses. He is without question more famous than his business.

Like him or not, he is a genius at attaching his name to anything and thereby associating that product with luxury. This opulence is immediately identifiable, whether a hotel, commercial office building, casino, television show or any number of diverse products.

Donald deliberately steps into the spotlight. He is adept at creating attention and is very comfortable in his own skin and hair. His tremendous success is based on his wide-spread exposure.

Donald Trump is the Logo.

Steve Jobs

Steve Jobs needs no introduction. His legend and legacy are larger than life.

During his two tenures as Apple's CEO, Steve became synonymous with the product and of services his company. In fact, he was – and is – as famous as the Apple brand itself.

One didn't have to be an Apple customer to recognize that Steve was a technology superstar and celebrity. Many refer to him as the best CEO the world has ever seen. Every time he held a press conference to launch a new product or to make an announcement, the world paid attention.

"What will Steve Jobs do next?" the papers, blogs, and public asked, as often (if not more) as they asked, "What will Apple do next?"

Steve Jobs and Apple were synonymous. Every item that Apple produced had to pass his rigorous approval. His unflinching requirement for excellence became the catalyst of one of the world's most valuable and respected companies.

He was the real Logo for Apple. Steve was the inspirational example of what it means to be the Logo of a product-focused company.

Steve Jobs was the Logo.

Tony Hawk

Tony Hawk is a legend in the skateboard parks and video game world. Tony has been a professional skateboarder from the time he was 14 and is the most awarded skateboard athlete in history. He is the first skateboarder to ever land a "900" which is 2.5 revolutions or 900 degree aerial spin performed on a skateboard ramp. Tony's passion for skateboarding led him to start a skateboard company called Birdhouse Projects.

In the early 90's, when the skateboarding culture died, Tony persevered as the Logo. As skateboarding rebounded, Tony was in position to be not only his business Logo, but the personal icon for the entire skateboarding industry.

Birdhouse, his first business grew into the biggest and best-known skateboard company in the world. Tony signed numerous endorsement deals. He teamed up with Activision to create the Tony Hawk Pro Skater video game franchise that has become one of the most popular video games in history.

Tony continues to leverage his personal Logo to launch even more businesses.

Tony Hawk is The Logo.

Oprah

Oprah doesn't need any explanation. Oprah doesn't even need a last name. She is a force in entertainment and in business as well. As the CEO of Harpo, Oprah runs an empire that includes TV shows, magazines and more recently, a partnership in her OWN network.

She has evolved as the Logo in a very different way than the others previously listed. Oprah built her name first as a reporter and then as a talk show host. Along the way, she established her reputation as someone who related with her audience.

She had many of the same struggles as they did. Oprah has a genuine concern and interest in people. She gives her viewers hope. Behind the scenes, she had been building a powerful business, which reinforced her very public persona.

Oprah Winfrey is The Logo.

I could fill this book with many more Logo stories. The following are familiar to us all:

Lee Iacocca, the Logo who saved Chrysler in the 1980's.

Joan Rivers, comedian, talk show host and TV personality. She continues to be the Logo for her many ventures.

Dave Thomas, the founder and CEO of Wendy's. Dave was known for appearing as the Logo in more than 800 commercial advertisements for Wendy's restaurants from 1989 to 2002, more than any other person in TV history.

Victor Kiam liked the Remington shaver so much, he bought the company. He served as its Logo for many years.

Martha Stewart, TV personality, magazine publisher, author and the Logo for her business enterprise, Omnimedia.

Michael Dell, as a pre-med student started selling upgrade kits for personal computers. This led to a number of variations of "storeless" direct computer sales and then to Dell Computer Corporation. While not as large an icon as some others, he remains the Logo for Dell to this day.

Mary Kay Ash, the founder of Mary Kay Cosmetics, was the icon to hundreds of thousands of women who built their own businesses selling the beauty and body care products.

I could go on: Wally "Famous" Amos, The Cookie Man; Calvin

Klein and Ralph Lauren, designers; Mark Cuban, the founder of MicroSolutions, Broadcast.com and the owner of the Dallas Mavericks; Warren Buffett, financial investor; Joel Osteen, the mega church pastor; Steve Forbes, publisher and politician; Norm Brodsky, author and founder of CitiStorage.

There is ample proof in this list that dynamic people can lead their companies to greatness using the power of their individual selves as the iconic, living Logo for their businesses.

But, I'm Not Like Them

I suspect as you read the previous list you might be thinking that these people are rich and powerful. They run large mega-corporations. They are different. They have it better than you.

Or perhaps you might be thinking that each person on the list of Logo examples is extraordinarily gifted and that's what truly gave them their success.

I encourage you to research each of these people and read their story. You will discover that they all started out in pretty much the same way you and I have. They built a business. Some may have had the financial support of friends and family, while others bootstrapped it.

Each built something from nothing, or took something that someone else developed and made it better. What makes all of them unique is that they deliberately chose to be fully in the spotlight.

Instead of mentioning only the big name, well-known Logos, here are some examples of other business professionals you might feel represent you more accurately.

Gary Vaynerchuk

Gary started working in his family's wine and liquor store in Springfield, New Jersey, at a very young age. While in high school, he started reading *Wine Spectator* as well as books on the subject of wine.

Soon he gained an incredible appreciation for the allure of collecting wines.

After college, as Gary was working full-time in the store, he began to recognize the Internet opportunity that was unfolding. As a result he started an online e-commerce site called WineLibrary.com and helped grow his family's business from $3 million in revenue to $45 million by 2005. He then launched WineLibraryTV.com, an online video blog that changed the wine world and launched him into the stratosphere.

Gary has been described as the wine guru to the YouTube generation. If you have ever watched his show, you will know that he is deeply passionate about wine and people. Gary has gone on to launch his own speaking and consulting empire as well as landing a major book deal.

Gary Vaynerchuk… You Are The Logo!

Christine Magee

Sleep Country Canada is Canada's largest and most well-known mattress retail chain. Standing front and center is its President and Co-founder, Christine Magee.

The co-founders of the chain were very strategic about making Christine the Logo for the business. Gord Lownds, former CEO of Sleep Country Canada, explains how important it was to have Christine as the personality promoting the business.

> "I think it was significant for a couple of reasons. Most of the people who make decisions about mattress purchases are women – about 75 to 80 per cent. Furthermore, Christine is not a hired model spokesperson, but a legitimate businessperson. And I think people recognize her for that. From a marketing point of view, I think people like to see a successful female running a business with some responsibility. Christine is also trustworthy, and it's all about building trust with the consumer."

Christine Magee… You are The Logo!

Dr. Greg Neilson

Dr. Greg Neilson is a chiropractor in Waterford, Wisconsin, a town of about 2,000 people. He provides health care services to his community and has done so for more than 20 years.

Dr. Neilson's direct mail marketing is world-renowned for being innovative, funny and interesting. He uses what he calls "Soap Opera Marketing." He has created something so interesting and phenomenal in his marketing that instead of the 2% customary response, Dr. Neilson regularly gets 20-30% response on his direct mail.

Direct marketers from many other disciplines actually pay to be on his mailing list just to see what he sends each month.

His very unique approach to being the Logo for his chiropractic business has created a professional service that is always full with a waiting list.

Dr. Greg Neilson... You Are The Logo!

Jim Penman

Jim's Group started as a part-time gardening and lawn mowing business in Australia while Jim Penman completed his PhD in History. It became a full-time business in 1982 and the first franchise was sold in 1989. Currently, there are over 2,900 franchises in four countries. Growing at the rate of around 200 per year, Jim's Group is one of the largest franchise companies in the world and is still run by its founder and Logo, Jim Penman.

Although he describes himself as someone extremely unlikely to build a successful business because of his poor management skills, social ineptitude and introversion, Jim Penman built his business on a refusal to give up, and, more importantly, on a belief that he could sell by not selling.

He has kept his face front and center over the years. Still to this day, with a huge franchise base that provides a wide range services including gardening, bookkeeping, antenna installations and even dog washing, Jim remains the ever present iconic personality of the business.

Jim Penman… You Are The Logo!

Bill Glazer

Bill Glazer entered his father's menswear business, Gage Menswear, in Baltimore, Maryland. When he took over the business, Bill believed there must be a better way to market his business. Bill Glazer recreated his stores into a menswear powerhouse and his two stores attained the highest revenue per square foot in North America. Bill was awarded the prestigious RAC Award at the Retail Advertising Conference, which is the retail equivalent of the Academy Award's Oscar.

Bill was all about outrageous advertising and was always doing something unique and interesting. He embedded himself as the personality icon for the business. He was so successful that he eventually sold the stores so that he could spend his time teaching others the secrets of his retail success.

Bill Glazer… You Are The Logo!

Become The Public Marketing Face of Your Business

There are many more stories of everyday business people who engage a "You Are The Logo" style of marketing to attract and engage their prospects. You will see more of them throughout the book.

As I have shown, there is substantial proof that the marketing strategy that elevates the owner or executive of a business to the role of public marketing icon can be one that is mimicked by you for your own success. The remainder of the book will provide the why and the how.

My hope is that you now believe that this "You Are The Logo" approach is a very proven and effective marketing methodology.

Prospective customers need a person (YOU!) to be the representation of the services they are buying. They need you to be the face and voice of the services and products you are selling, just like Donald, Steve and Oprah.

CHAPTER 2

A Better Way

There's a way to do it better – find it.
Thomas A. Edison

The decision to change your marketing approach is only appropriate if what you are currently doing is not working for you. If you are frustrated by your current situation and the results you are getting in response, you might be experiencing some or all of the following symptoms.

You Don't Stand Out From The Competition

If I asked you to remove your business logo from your brochure or website and replace it with one of your competitors, would your prospects actually be able to know the difference? Would there be anything that really separates you from your competitor?

A funny thing happens when we do business in competitive industries. We begin to look like our competitors. Instead of trying to do something completely different, we almost unknowingly replicate our competition and the way they market themselves. It's a condition that comes from looking at them much more than is necessary. And the more we look at what they do and say, the more it influences how we market ourselves. As a result, we don't stand out. We don't occupy a clear, unique and advantageous position in our prospective marketplace. In fact, to a prospect, everyone looks the same.

You Want Powerful Competitive Positioning

Powerful positioning means you emerge to become conspicuous from all the other competitors. In the sea of sameness you are overt and obviously different from all other vendors. You occupy a distinguished role in the industry or community you serve and as a result, you don't look like everyone else. When you talk to prospects, you provide them a clear and obvious reason to do business with you – and they take notice.

You Get Forced Into Commodity Comparisons

Competitive offerings of undifferentiated products or services that offer little or no perceived difference require the prospective buyer to reduce their method of comparison to only one thing, *price*. They have no other option. If all you offer as a vendor or service provider is almost identical to what they see from everyone else, then you will remain locked into the commodity comparison. Your only way to survive is to lower your price and increase your volume, a long-term recipe for disaster. The inevitable result of this commodity path is frustration.

Someone will always be willing and able to offer a lower price than you. And yet, so many believe this is the only way to ensure they survive.

You don't want to remain in the commodity comparison and pricing trap.

You Want Clients To Willingly Pay Your True Worth

The purchase of goods and services at the lowest price possible is never a wise business decision. Other than an extremely small percentage of those who have no other choice, buying decisions are made based on a complex array of criteria that often favor paying more to ensure better value.

When you get out of commodity comparisons, you open yourself up to a world where clients and customers are willing to pay significantly more – even premium amounts for things they consider valuable to them.

A few months ago, my dentist informed me that I needed to get a dental implant and crown to replace a tooth that had finally broken completely after a root canal 20 years ago. This required me to see a dental surgeon. In my conversations with my dentist, never once did I ask him to recommend the cheapest surgeon available. No, instead we talked about the most advanced and up-to-date methods for implants, which would mean only one surgery instead of the two typically required. He also suggested the very best dental surgeons who were specialists in this new implant technology. In exchange for better surgeons and better methods I was willing to pay premium prices.

You Seem Invisible In The Marketplace

How is it that your competitors actually won that RFP? How is it that you didn't even get to submit a bid? You weren't even on the list. How is it that you see announcements and press releases from competitors proclaiming their new business relationship with a client? You never even got a shot at it. Somehow the clients knew about your competitors, while you weren't even on their radar.

There is nothing worse than being invisible in your marketplace. Despite your best efforts, you are not getting the new business opportunities that are actually available. Your current approach does not help you get noticed.

You Want Enhanced Visibility and a Definitive Reputation

You want to be the company that everyone in your market is already aware of. You are highly visible. If there is an opportunity, your name comes up. Even if they don't choose to hire you, they at least give you a shot at the business. It's not just because of your enhanced visibility, it's because your reputation always precedes you. Opportunities for new business come to you based on referrals from existing clients and the reputation you've created within your marketplace.

You Lose Deals You Know You Should Be Winning

There is the tremendous frustration that comes when you do finally get a shot at those business opportunities and the prospect ends up going with the big, established "gorilla." Despite your certainty that the client will get less than stellar service from the other company, you can't ever seem to win those battles.

There are the times you lose out to competitors, not because you don't have the capability or even comparative pricing, you just don't have that little extra "something" to get the close ones. You somehow get passed over in these opportunities and you can never get a clear indication why. It seems that every competitive situation you enter seems stacked in your competitor's favor, not yours. Everyone else seems to possess the upper hand.

You Want To Have An Unfair Advantage

In business, it pays to have an unfair advantage and be the dominant force in your marketplace. When this occurs, you get the lion's share of the opportunity. Couple it with your ability to occupy the preferred vendor status in competitive situations and your strength becomes unmatched. When you hold this favored position you are like a world champion athlete competing at a high school level.

In these advantageous situations, the business comes your way even on the close ones. But the real unfairness happens when your competitors don't even get a chance at the business you obtain. Your positioning, visibility and reputation exclude them from even competing.

You Exist in "Wait and See" or "Hunt and Chase" Mode

If you passively "wait and see" whether or not clients call or walk in your door, you are in a terribly difficult situation. Hope is not a great strategy when it comes to getting new clients.

Alternatively, many sales-oriented industries rely on the "hunt and chase" model to get the job done. The salesperson determines where to find new leads. They are encouraged to hunt and chase target prospects. Once the quarry is cornered, the salesperson is required to close the deal. You know the drill.

Many years ago I worked for a consulting firm. Cold calling was the prescribed method for new consultants to generate business. I'd sit and look at call lists all day long that were assigned me, then pick up the phone and dial through the list. After I left enough messages, I would wait and see who would call back. If I got any small indication of interest, the hunt and chase would happen.

I discovered that this approach worked against me, not for me. I was "an interruption" in their day. I became an unwelcome pest, instead of a welcome guest. Occasionally, I got lucky, but mostly I just spun my wheels.

When you chase your prospects, you instantly reduce your value. At its very core, it is confrontational and adversarial. The perception on the part of the prospect is that you need to do business with them. Hunting and chasing is not the way you want to be known by prospective clients.

You Want Magnetic Marketing That Provides a Steady Stream Of Business

In most instances, business leaders demand hunting from themselves or from their sales team because they are unable or unwilling to invest the considerable time and effort required to develop the appropriate type of marketing that makes hunting and chasing completely unnecessary.

In my consulting job, I noticed a very different methodology employed by Marvin Haggith, the owner and principal of the firm. He didn't make cold calls, yet he took a steady stream of calls from prospective clients. Marvin had an attraction system that seemed counter to what he was asking me to do as a new recruit. While I chased and waited, he continued to obtain new and returning clients almost magnetically.

Magnetic marketing ensures your most likely prospects know who you are, what you do and why they should do business with you. You are not a stranger to them. You are a known entity. You are liked and trusted. When they are ready, they take the initiative, already prepared, pre-disposed and willing to do business with you. So, instead of chasing them or waiting for them, they come to you. As a result the context for the sales discussion is changed dramatically.

You Are Compared On The Wrong Criteria

If the services you offer – or deliverables your business provides –are the only basis for comparison by your clients, you will inevitably fall back into the trap of commoditization and the inability to stand out. If what you *do* is what you rely on to make the eventual sale, you will always face undue competitive pressure and comparison with anyone else who does it too. After all, anyone can claim to do the same work you do even with varying degrees of quality.

If my company builds websites, than any other company that builds websites is the basis of competitive comparison by a potential customer.

I can say we provide "great service," but so can my competitor. I can spout terms like "excellence," "solutions" and "customer-centric" and so can my competitors. I can even enhance my position by confirming some even more unique things like how long I've been in business and how we have great systems for building websites.

In the end, the comparison is still focused on things that allow a prospect to set up a comparative spreadsheet. They are all items that can be compared. And you don't want to be in that comparison situation.

You Want To Be Chosen Based on Who You Are Not What You Do

In my consulting job outlined previously, I eventually discovered the secret to the Marvin Haggith's success... Him. He got the business and was paid handsomely for it – because of *who* he was – more than for *what* he actually did. Granted, he was very good at what he did, but there were countless other companies in the market who provided a comparable suite of services to what his firm offered.

What Marvin provided his client was something the competitors could not: his story, his history, his set of connections, his insider knowledge and his definitive reputation. It was this uniqueness that gave Marvin an unfair advantage in the market.

For Marvin, the "who" he sold ultimately mattered more than the "what" he sold. It should be the same for you too.

I believe the most powerful way for you to:

- stand out from your competition
- be positioned powerfully
- remove yourself from the commodity trap
- get paid for your real value
- move from invisibility to a definitive reputation
- get out of the hunt and chase game, and
- magnetically attract a steady stream of business

is to leverage... **YOU!**

You are the catalyst to create the attraction, the positioning and the reputation that will be a force for your business success in your market. And this book will show you how.

CHAPTER 3

The Time Is Now

*I take a simple view of life:
keep your eyes open and get on with it.*
Sir Laurence Olivier

Our current environment is positioned for You – not your brand – to be the Logo for your business. Here are some of the key factors that make the timing so right.

The Rage Against The 1%

Look no further than the last few years to see the impact of big banks, Wall Street, phone and automobile conglomerates and the damage they've done to the once proud corporate reputations. It's hard *not* to find greed near the top.

The Occupy Movement first sprung up in 2011. This grassroots organization has made a very vocal statement, not just in the U.S., but around the world. The angry sentiment is leveled at corporations and those executives who run them.

Robert Scoble and Shel Israel in their book, *Naked Conversations* say this:

> "We live in a time where most people don't trust big companies. Headlines gush with tales of malfeasance, abuse, and old fashioned plunder, but that's just part of the problem. There's a general perception that large companies are run by slick lawyers and book fixing accountants who oversee armies of obedient, drone like employees. Companies are perceived as monoliths without souls. In short we see NO humanity."

It is in this corporate environment where a wonderful opportunity emerges for you to stand out in stark contrast. Instead of hiding behind the "Corporation" – even a small, private one – you can position yourself dramatically, fundamentally and squarely opposite them as one who exhibits humanity and soul.

It's about putting yourself out there as the public name and face of your business in stark contrast to a marketplace full of nameless, faceless, soul-less companies. It's about showing and sharing *you*. It's about being a business leader with skin on.

Real people in business ownership and leadership are what prospects are attracted to. This is what the market is craving.

It's A Facebook World

If the explosive growth of Facebook over the last few years has proven a point; it is that we crave the human connection, even if it is virtual.

Today's clients and customers want and need to have a personal, human connection to someone within the context of the services they are getting.

While this human connection can be provided to them on the actual delivery of the services you offer, it is even more important that there be a very visible human connection in the upfront marketing of your business. It's a significant factor that attracts them to your business in the first place.

The adoption of social media around the world has more than proven this point. In an insulated, high tech, sit-in-front-of-your-screen kind of world, a very real social relationship is critical to today's success regardless of the nature of your business.

You cannot afford to miss this point. People are *not* social with a brand. They are social with other people. They talk *about* brands but they talk *to* people. There's a huge difference.

This new way of marketing your business (one that puts you "front and center" as the owner or executive) aligns with the present culture.

In 2011, a study was conducted to determine why Facebook elicits such an emotional response in people. NeuroFocus, the organization that did the study, wired the research participants with EEG sensors to measure their brainwave patterns while they visited Facebook and other sites.

In response to the study, A. K. Pradeep, the CEO of NeuroFocus explained that the presence of faces on Facebook was the major reason why the emotional engagement was so high.

> "As you can see, one of the dominant features of Facebook is the human face," he says. "The face is a window to the emotions."

Pradeep says that since childhood we are trained to read people's faces to discern emotion, and that such information is key to survival. This accounts for the stimulation we experience when scanning our social news feeds.

The point I want you to take from this is that your face *matters* because it actually launches an emotional response in your prospects. In a social media world, your presence and your face, as the representation of your business, are emotional Velcro.

While I am not discussing the merits of using Facebook or any other social media platform as a marketing tactic, I do want to impress upon you that if your business is dependent on traditional brand messaging formulas that try to exist without a personal, social approach to marketing, you are fighting a steep, uphill battle that is in opposition to the current social culture.

Reality Voyeurs

As a nation we are seduced by *The Housewives of Beverly Hills* and *Orange County* and *New Jersey*. We can't seem to get enough of the bizarre and strange family lives and escapades of *The Kardashians*. We are emotionally grabbed by the life transformations of *The Biggest Losers*. We find ourselves auditioning with and struggling to rise to the adulation of an *American Idol*. The list goes on. Start flicking through your channels any night of the week and you will begin to see how "reality" TV has transformed the small screen.

It seems like every other TV show is focused on "reality." We now have the ability to glimpse into their world and observe what's happening in their lives. When we add the impact and "reality" of the billions of minutes of YouTube videos that are uploaded and watched every day, we realize that "reality" is the norm.

Even though we all know that it's not truly "reality" since there are cameras involved, our culture has still shifted to an almost obsessive interest in "reality" entertainment. This is the world in which we are marketing our businesses. Whether you like it or not, or even agree or not, the point remains that people today want reality entertainment.

They want to see the truth of you and your business. They don't want the Madison Avenue glossy, fake façade that seems to present a veneer of pretty, pleasing and perfect corporate-speak whitewashed by marketing machines.

I am not suggesting that you create a reality show for your business. Duff Goldman of *Charm City Cakes* has done okay for himself as a result of his business reality show. Many others including self storage auction buyers, pawn shop brokers, custom motorcycle and car shop owners, bounty hunters, and even tow truck drivers have also made names for themselves on TV.

If you choose to take this path, you have the opportunity to share yourself and your business in a very real way. The goal of reality is never perfection. It's a willingness to expose the good, the bad and the ugly to an audience that is hungry for it.

Celebrity Obsession

While we seem to love watching the reality of the lives of others, the media and its consumers seem positively obsessed with celebrity.

The world watches celebrities from film, TV and music as well as the pseudo-celebrities from the reality shows, to know what they are doing. *TMZ* and *Entertainment Tonight*, even Oprah herself, support our ability to get to know the celebrities and see what they are doing.

The fact is that we think we want their lives. We want what they have. We want the dream and the apparent rewards that come with it. These celebrities are presented as ordinary folks like us in almost every way. The major difference is that they live in a very different world and it makes our lives and ways seem woefully dull by comparison.

Your customers and prospects are pre-disposed to being attracted to celebrity. They want to connect with a story bigger than their own, even if only by observation.

Leveraging this reality in your marketing efforts can be a beneficial thing. No, I'm not suggesting you try to get on TV with the type of celebrity status that gets *TMZ* reporters and paparazzi following your every step. You don't need *that* much celebrity. However, you have a celebrity story at your disposal.

The birth and growth of your business is worthy of adulation. You've done something in building a business that millions of others have not done or even tried. You should use it to your advantage.

A Need For Heroes

While reality voyeurism and celebrity obsession seem less than noble, scratch the surface of most people and you'll discover that all of us want a hero in our lives. If we worship celebrities out of a desire to have their lives and their privilege, we need heroes because they symbolize the qualities we'd like to possess. We aspire to their noble achievements.

Heroes are generally known for their courage, bravery or the willingness to take risks. They accomplish things that few others would ever wish to attempt.

Ralph Waldo Emerson wrote, "A hero is no braver than an ordinary man, but he is brave five minutes longer." These five extra minutes of bravery translate into the hero's ability to teach, inspire us to greatness and captivate us with their deeds.

As a business owner, your story is a hero's journey.

In his seminal book *The Hero With A Thousand Faces*, Joseph Campbell described a basic pattern found in most narratives around the world. Campbell lists 17 stages in the journey, which can be divided into three basic sections.

The first is "Departure" which deals with the hero's struggle prior to the quest. It includes the call to adventure signifying the destiny the hero is called to undergo, the refusal to heed that internal call, and the crossing of the threshold into the reality of the adventure.

As business owners or entrepreneurs, we have engaged our own departure. We have at some point felt the desire and inner callings to start a business, fraught with so much peril. We resist for a time, but we eventually make the leap into the unknown of this journey.

The second section of Campbell's book describes the "Initiation." This is the phase in which the hero must go through a series of trials, tests, tasks and ordeals that creates a powerful transformation in the hero.

My business journey includes tests, trials, overwhelming tasks and ordeals on a daily basis. If you own or run a business, you easily fit into this section of the hero's journey.

However, the hero's journey is not truly complete until the hero returns to share the knowledge and powers acquired on the journey to the benefit of others. In this third phase, called the "Return," the hero brings the gifts gained from the journey back to his or her community.

As a business owner or executive, I want you to know that the world *needs* you to be a hero. You will experience the journey as outlined here, but where it matters most is when you can be the person who brings something better back to the world. Your business is a catalyst to bring value to the world.

At my point of "Departure" I was a rookie store manager for a large regional chain of traditional menswear stores. I had been appointed Manager because I had been willing to work extra hours and shifts when others didn't. I had no experience in the business world as my training and experience up to that point was as a Music Pastor. One day my District Manager invited me to lunch and asked if I would be willing to take a huge risk and start a new, exciting menswear business together. After considerable uncertainty, I took the plunge.

There were plenty of "Initiation" events in the years to follow. One store turned into seven, and then seven stores turned back into one. I could write a book about the lessons learned during the amazing growth of that business – and the harsh reality of losing it all. But the rise and fall of Jordan's Menswear taught me many enduring lessons and provided me with a war chest of knowledge that became lessons to share in my "Return." Those gifts were ones I have carried forward, allowing me to help so many others in their journeys as a consultant and guide.

Return to Small Town Thinking

In a world that is global and complex, people want to go back to simplicity. They want to go back to a time where life is about knowing people and being known. They want a place where they can walk out their front door and talk to their neighbors. It's a place where they can walk uptown, and stop and say "Hello" to the owner of the local grocery store. Most importantly, they want the owner of the store to recognize and respond to them by name.

In his latest speeches and books, Gary Vaynerchuk has helped many people understand the new reality in which we now live. His point being: we exist in a social environment where everyone posts and tweets and have access to our entire social lives, we've returned to small town rules.

Having grown up in small towns, I know that the relationship and its value was everything. Deals were done on handshakes because each party knew the other. Background checks weren't needed. The proprietor knew your order and your preferences, and was often willing to run you a tab.

I am not so naïve as to believe that the whole business world will get back to that type of existence. However, I am convinced that in your world and business, if you start to engage and act consistent with this small town philosophy, you will see some incredibly cool things happen.

Today I live in San Diego, one of the largest cities in North America. I live next door to people I've never met and might never meet. Within blocks of me are tens of thousands of people. Yet, something about life in the city seems to have removed our humanity. As I walk down the street and pass people, we make no eye contact and exchange no greetings. Still, I am convinced that secretly we all want to be greeted by others. We want to be noticed and recognized.

I believe this because, on the rare occasion that it does happen, people who are stiff, guarded and reserved, suddenly become full of life. They are energized and communicative when they are recognized by someone on the street or in the store.

I was shopping during the holidays. Having lost my small town willingness to chat with everyone I meet, I entered a store and remained a quiet visitor. As I was browsing through the store I heard her. She spoke to me from behind a display cabinet.

"You're the Sunday latte guy!"

"Huh?" I replied. I was confused.

After some initial back and forth, I realized she was the barista at the coffee shop I visit every Sunday morning before I do my weekly grocery shopping. This connection with her changed the energy of the moment. I was transformed from a lone shopper to an emotionally engaged person.

As a business owner or executive, we have the power to change the environment, and, as a result, change the nature of our business interactions. Your clients want to be known. They also want to know you. Today, more than ever, they need it as well.

The queen of all media is Oprah Winfrey. Oprah discovered a magic formula. By building a relationship with her audience, she ensured that they would never leave her. She never talked down to her viewers and always presented stories that were relevant to their lives. She built and maintained a trusting relationship with her TV audience in the 25 years she had her daily talk show. This formula helped her build an empire.

Today's customers and clients trust certain brands, but they don't always build relationships with them. When Steve Jobs stepped down as CEO of Apple, the world shed a collective tear for the man they felt they had come to know personally.

Customers and clients build better relationships with people. They build better relationships with you… not brands. They grow to trust people.

There has never been a better, more opportune time for you to be the Logo for your business. The planets are aligned in such a way that stepping in to this very visible marketing role as your company's personality marketer can be a significant transformative act for your business.

CHAPTER 4

Some Marketing Refreshers

*Marketing is too important to be left
to the marketing department.*
David Packard

In this chapter, let's look more closely at some of the most important marketing concepts. These are fundamental to You Are The Logo marketing.

You Are First and Foremost A Marketer

As the face of your business, your job is to be the marketer for your business. This is your primary objective. "This is your mission, should you choose to accept it."

One of the significant transitions you must make in your thinking is to rid yourself of the belief that you are in the business that you think you are in.

Multi-millionaire entrepreneur and marketing advisor Dan Kennedy, has been an incredible guide to me in this area. He suggests that you are primarily in the business of marketing and selling the services you provide, and not in the delivery of those services. Marketing is your highest calling.

> **I AM FIRST A MARKETER**

Everything you do during the workday and beyond is designed and intended to promote your business. That's the sign you need to place on the screen saver on your computer. You don't have to put it on your business card, but being the marketer for your company is what you will do day in and day out. It's your new calling.

Choose A Select Group of Somebodys

One of the fundamental mistakes that so many make is that they try to market to the whole world. If you are in the janitorial business, you tend to believe that every business in the city could use your services.

The problem is that you can never create an iconic status or presence with every business. You probably don't have the financial pockets to ensure it happens. You don't have the ability to build a strong enough marketing machine to get in front of the entire market.

However, if you made a decision to be the janitorial company that serviced medical offices, which required HIPAA and HITECH compliance, you have now created a marketplace niche. With that one tiny "niche-ification" of your business, you will be considered a solid and valuable provider.

My company, Flourish Press, has spent the last eight years highly focused on a relatively small industry in the world. As we have targeted on servicing this very small niche, it has allowed all sorts of advantages in both the marketing and servicing of clients. We have a clearly defined list of prospects. Marketing has become much easier.

Ben Glass is a lawyer based in Virginia. More specifically, he is a "Fairfax, Virginia, Car Accident and Medical Malpractice Attorney." If that isn't a niche, I don't know what is, but it works for him. If he had been trying to be a general lawyer, he wouldn't get nearly the same results.

Your goal may be to become the most sought-after Certified Public Accountant in your city but you are going to have a huge battle to get there. On the other hand, if you became the CPA of choice for all the veterinarians in town, you now have an opportunity to make something happen. The competition is fierce for the masses. You don't want to be there. If you don't find your niche, you're simply a small fish in a big pond. Your goal is to be a big fish in a very small pond. And the only way to do that is to reduce your market. You need to shrink your prospect world to a place where you are the ONLY one who does what you do.

You will stand out in the crowd when you find your niche. Targeting a special client or customer group lets you speak directly to the exact needs they have in their unique situations.

Offer Services That Align With Niche Requirements

Business revenue and profit are the results of providing goods or services, which have perceived value to your marketplace. If you've effectively established your target niche, and offer services that create a perceived high value to your niche prospects and customers, you will have a highly effective business.

Your services can be structured to respond to the problems, predicaments or pain that your niche deals with. You begin to understand how your service creates a unique opportunity for you to charge premium prices to your clients. You become comfortable speaking their language, not just your own.

Implement Persistent Campaigns To Your Niche

Effective marketing is the practice of putting your message and business offers in front of your prospects on a regular and recurring basis.

Marketing for many companies is perceived as an event. We "did" a direct mail campaign. We "produced" a flyer. We "made" some cold calls. We "held" a lunch-and-learn training session. We "exhibited" at a trade show. All of these activities are good tactics, but as single events they do not produce the results you require.

To be effective, you must transition your thinking from event-based to campaign-based marketing.

Imagine you are running for political office and your goal is to get elected in two years. Everything you do today – and for the next two years – will help decide the result in the election. Therefore, you don't do something once – you do it repeatedly. You don't run one ad. Instead, you run many ads over the course of your campaign all designed to achieve a connection with a specific type of voter. You don't send mail once; you send different campaigns to different people. You don't do one interview; you do them all over your constituency so that you get the optimal amount of coverage. You don't do one speech and hope they remember it; you speak every opportunity you can.

Marketing is just a day in, day out, never ending persevering kind of activity. To be truly effective, you must think of your marketing as an entire campaign.

Ensure A Ubiquity of Presence

Be everywhere for your prospects. Show up like nobody else.

If you understand the power of a niche and the value of campaigning, you begin to create a presence. So it will seem to your prospects like you are everywhere. You will be perceived as being ubiquitous.

The goal is not just being everywhere. The goal is being there when they decide they need you. They need to see you, hear you, and talk to you, even before they decide they want to do business with you. If you're a phantom, your chances for success are doomed.

Develop a plan to get your face, name and voice out there consistently and repeatedly as the Logo for your business.

Integrate Multiple Marketing Elements

If you only do one or two of the strategies that I am outlining in this book you're shutting out most of your new potential business. You must do more than just write an article or do a radio commercial.

Author Jay Abraham talks about the Power Parthenon of Geometric Business Growth. He suggests that if you have one source of marketing, such as cold calling or newspaper advertising, your business is vulnerable to instability. But if you have 10 ways to acquire a new customer, you have increased your stability. If you have 20 ways to connect with and market to your prospects, you are in a powerful marketing position. Diversity in your marketing tactics leads to economic stability.

You'll want to make it your goal to engage as many of the tactics that you can comfortably and effectively use to solidify your marketing presence.

Reuse and Recycle Your Marketing

To become more efficient in all your marketing, aim to reuse and recycle your marketing assets and collateral materials. When you do something, consider how you might repurpose or adapt it for things. For example:

- Record the speech or conference session you are presenting and post it online or burn it to a DVD video for physical distribution.
- Get a copy of your media interviews and add them to your website as a streaming audio or video file.
- Recycle the article you write for your newsletter as a guest post on someone else's blog.
- Copy and reprint the articles that are written about you (or that include you) as part of a promotional kit.

In my own experience I have repurposed materials many times. I record every speech by audio and add it to my website so it can be heard again. Every article I have written for an external publication is reused as support material in business proposals or adapted for my own company newsletter. Ads or direct mail pieces for one audience are adapted to suit another audience. This "recycling" has allowed me to have an endless reserve of resources to draw from as I engage new campaigns.

Reusing your marketing assets will not only save you time and resources on the creation of new materials, it will also provide an archive of credibility to retain and share as you market in the future.

Go Beyond Your Comfort Zone

The goal of marketing is to produce a consistent set of leads and clients coming to your business. If your marketing isn't working, you need to change it. Break out of your routine. Take a risk on something new and different. Effective marketing requires you – as the leader of the business – to do something very different than what you have been doing.

Before we get into the actual methodologies you can implement in your own version of *You Are The Logo* marketing, I will outline some characteristics you will need to embrace in order to best engage this type of marketing.

✶ CHAPTER 5 ✶

The "You" Required

*Don't just express yourself, invent yourself.
And don't restrict yourself to off the shelf models.*
Henry Louis Gates, Jr.

A ll of this boils down to just one thing... *you*. We're not discussing how to assemble a marketing team, jump-start your cold calling efforts or write brochures – we're talking about you becoming the personality marketer for your business.

You have it inside of you. It's like a tiny seed that just needs some water, a little sun and some soil to grow. You already have what it takes to become the person you never thought you could be. This chapter looks at the You needed to become that person.

I've observed the most successful personalities. These industry leaders, business heroes, and everyday business owners who wanted to try something different all had some characteristics worth noting. I've found through my own experience, as well as those of my clients, what it takes to be the personality for your business.

Be Yourself

In this process, we need to find *you*. You must now do some introspective searching.

Ask yourself the following questions:

- What are your strengths?
- What are your weaknesses?
- What are your pet peeves?
- Who are your enemies?
- What made you get into your business in the first place?
- What draws others to you?
- What turns them away?

When you answer these and many other questions honestly, you will get to the root of who you are. You will see your identity. This is what we'll be working with.

> *Be yourself because everyone else is already taken.*
> Oscar Wilde

Oprah Winfrey certainly makes no qualms about who she is. She's shared her darkest secrets and her greatest joys with the audience. The person we see on TV is an authentic Oprah Winfrey. As your business's marketing personality, you will be showing the real you. There can be no substitutes.

In You Are The Logo marketing, your uniqueness is important. Everything about you – including your eccentricity, mannerisms, lame jokes, style, and even your fashion sense – can be an asset. Don't look at other people and try to be them.

The world doesn't need any more Martha Stewarts, Gary Vaynerchuks or Christine Magees. It needs people with unique, individual perspectives and personalities. It needs you to be **you**. And the best way to be you is to embrace and share your story.

You Are Your Story

We all love a good story. In fact, it is hardwired into our nature as humans to listen to them. Our entire history revolves around the telling of stories.

It is highly important to have a well-developed story that you are ready, willing and able to share.

Warren Buffett has one of the best well-known "Logo" stories. You might have heard the "Oracle of Omaha" grew up in Depression-era Nebraska and started selling gum, Coca-Cola and magazines door-to-door. He set his sights on being a millionaire by 35. His dream started to become reality through Berkshire Hathaway, which grew out of small investment company funded mostly by family members. Buffett has told this story for years. It is told and retold because it provides backstory for his incredible success.

Ira Glass, host of the incredibly popular radio show, *This American Life*, believes in the power of story. His show has allowed listeners to get into the stories in a way that is almost impossible to resist. His 60-minute show gets an average 48 minutes of listening time, proving that his formula for telling stories works.

"Narrative is like a back door into a very deep place inside of us. And a place where reason doesn't necessarily hold sway," Glass suggests.

The world of marketing and sales is a place full of polished corporate speak and crafted lingo. It is often littered with features, benefits, advantages and hyperbole that have NO emotional connection. This type of communication engages your prospects, but only at a purely intellectual level with you as a vendor.

However, when you tell your story, something changes.

The Naked Accountant

Jean Carpenter Backus is a CPA and financial planning expert and guide in Austin, Texas. She is a founding Partner of Carpenter & Langford,

> "An accounting firm that provides quality of services demanded of the national firms with the close client relations expected of a local firm."

That explanation of her firm alone is not enough to make you interested, even remotely. It's great "copy" but it's not that attractive to most. You could take that statement and transpose it with any one of a thousand other accounting firms and you wouldn't know the difference.

Now, if you have a chance to hear Jean tell her story and share her experiences about her philosophy about money and finances, I am sure you would want to meet her. There is no "marketing speak" in her story. There is only an intense attraction.

When Jean tells her story of being an orphan, a high school dropout, a wife at 14 and a teen mom to a special needs child, you are hooked.

As Jean tells her story, she shares her philosophy and beliefs about financial management that make you want to pick up the phone and give her a call.

Tell Your Story

If you are going to become the Logo for your business, your story is a critical element in your toolkit. You piece together the elements of your story that will capture the essence of who you are and what you want your clients and prospects to know about you. You structure it in such a way so that the telling of it creates emotional connections to you, not just intellectual ones. These *emotional* connections are much more powerful.

Once you have your story laid out, stick to it. Remember that it's part of your identity. It's part of what makes you compelling. In fact, your personal story reinforces all of the things that you want to showcase, as opposed to the boring, corporate stuff that is so often the case.

Hidden in your "story" are the reasons why you do what you do. Your story is the birthplace of your passion for your work. So craft your story in a way that shows that your background and your success through qualities such as hard work, raw talent and commitment to your dreams. It makes you real. It makes you more attractive, authentic and interesting, not "corporate."

Exhibit Your Passion

Blake Mycoskie is a passionate guy. He built and sold five successful companies by the age of 32. Then, while on vacation in Argentina, he learned about a simple shoe program run by social workers that were trying to help shoeless children. These social workers found used shoes for the kids, but unfortunately, the shoes were ill-fitting and worn. As Blake learned more about the shoe problem in Argentina, he discovered that when children are shoeless, it not only affects their health but their ability to get an education as well. Children are not allowed to go to school if they are shoeless.

It was then that his entrepreneurial mind decided to create a business that would be a sustainable way to support the shoeless. This newly discovered passion dovetailed with his entrepreneurial instincts to create something pretty amazing. He created TOMS, a company dedicated to making and selling shoes. But the genius of his idea was to integrate charity into a for-profit business model as defined on Toms.com.

> "With every pair you purchase, TOMS will give a pair of new shoes to a child in need. One for One."

Blake's company continues to grow rapidly. The incredible part of this story is that as he shared his passion, it was contagiously adopted by others. First the story was spread by those who bought his shoes, then by larger firms, who further spread the word in an even bigger way. Thus, the story and his passion got passed along so much that today, while you might never have heard of Blake, you've likely heard of TOMS.

There are thousands of examples of people who have built businesses based on an existing passion of theirs. The food industry is full of businesses built around owners' passion to cook. There are those who love clothes and then open a retail store. Deep inside most small- to mid-sized business owners you will find that there is a passion for it.

Passionate About Fixing What's Wrong

Dr. Tom Lee is a primary care physician who wanted something different for patients. His desire to do this was born out of his own experiences as a patient, as well as his frustration with the medical system. This ignited in him a passionate desire to create memorable primary care experiences for his patients. So he built a practice, One Medical Group Inc., which was the expression of his passion.

Dr. Lee's passion has fueled the development of a medical practice that seeks to act more like a hotel and restaurant in terms of service and is supported by the operational efficiency more commonly found in the manufacturing industry. The tagline for *One Medical Group* is "Not Your Typical Doctor's Office."

It's obvious that his passion, now implemented, is working. His business is growing rapidly. An article in the *New York Times* stated that One Medical Group is growing at a rate of 50% per year.

A Passion to Succeed

Sometimes, there is no grand passion like Blake's, or even – a more defined passion – to support clients or patients as outlined by Dr. Lee. Sometimes, the passion of a business owner or entrepreneur is connected to the desire to succeed against the odds. Other times, it is to build something from nothing or create extraordinary profits.

Passion helped Ben and Jerry stick it out through the lean years scooping ice cream in a gas station to create a nationally successful confectionary business. Passion is what took Bill Hewlett and David Packard out of the shack and into the boardroom as they built the wildly successful Hewlett-Packard.

It's also the story of you, and thousands of others who have, against all odds, built a business that stands as a testament to that passion.

If you want to step into the limelight and lead the marketing charge for your business, you have to be passionate about what it is that you do in the world. You can't fake passion either. The ultra-savvy buyer today can smell counterfeit passion a mile away. Your passion must be genuine. Your passion is magnetic and attractive.

Activate Your Public Persona

A persona is the aspect of someone's character that is presented to others or is perceived by others. As the Logo for your business, your persona is something you should craft based on your story and the passion you feel. The question regarding persona is: "Who are you going to be?"

Not Your Typical TV Preacher

Joel Osteen, televangelist and senior pastor of the Lakewood Church, in Houston, Texas, has his critics. Although he's successful and reaches millions around the globe through his TV ministry and books, many still think he oversimplifies religion.

> *Life isn't about finding yourself.*
> *Life is about creating yourself.*
> George Bernard Shaw

However, part of Osteen's success is that he decided, long before he became famous, that his persona would be approachable and relatable, and that he was no different than his church members who themselves possess only an average understanding of theology.

His persona demonstrates encouragement, compassion and hope. Different than some TV preachers – who are all about the big antics or the ones that tug at your heartstrings for donations – Osteen comes across as your trusted neighbor, or as the friend you would call in a crisis. He seems like someone that you would enjoy having a cup of coffee with. And it's working for him.

Craft Your Persona

If you are going to elevate yourself to a more defined role in marketing your business, you need to craft the persona you are going to deliver publically.

Here is a list of some generalized personas to use as examples.

- The "make the world a better place" type. Your business is a way to change the world.
- The one to rescue clients from the treatment by others. A hero.
- The trusted friend and confidant – I've walked in your shoes and I'll help you too.
- The analyst who discovers things through research and development, by looking at things in a different way.
- The visionary who charts a new path to something better. You see things that others can't.
- The advisor or educator. You are all about teaching people a better way.
- The artist. It's more about creation and less about business.
- The no-BS, "tell it like it is" person. You confront the hypocrisy and speak the truth.
- The doer. You get it done. No hype, no fuss. You'll do it because they can't or don't want to.
- The old grizzled veteran who has experienced all the options and has come to a place where what you do still works.

This is not an inclusive list. There is an unlimited supply of options.

My point is, as you craft your unique public persona, you can't be everything. You can't be their best friend and trusted adviser and also be the rescuer, as well as the no BS person all at the same time. You'll confuse your customers.

The whole point of your persona is to use it in your marketing as a way to build a solid position. Once people have met you, they can decide if you are someone they like or dislike. If the goal is to attract clients, then you cannot be someone who produces indifferent reactions in your prospects. Your persona is what people gravitate to.

They'll listen to your story. They'll be impressed by your passion. However, they will "follow you" based on your persona.

The persona that I present in my own business is that of an advisor and educator, coupled with being a trusted friend and confidant. While there are times I take on certain characteristics of another persona, my primary persona is where I am most authentic with myself and my clients.

Authenticity Matters

The persona you choose must align with who you really are. If you adopting a persona that does not align with who you are to begin with, it won't ring true with customers.

A study found that the reputation of a CEO can greatly affect how his or her business is perceived. Inauthentic personalities are going to translate into a negative perception of your business. Stay authentic.

Become Visible

If you choose to implement a You Are The Logo style of marketing, you have to become visible. You have to tell your story and exemplify your passion. You must be a certain "kind of someone" as you express your unique persona in the world of your prospects and clients.

The world needs you to show up in a big way. Your presence, no matter what form it takes, will lead your company or business to a better place. So, don't sit quietly in your office wondering why your business isn't growing.

Get out there and BE the Logo.

CHAPTER 6

Craft Your Positioning

*Don't compromise yourself, honey.
You're all you've got.*
Janis Joplin

You Are The Logo marketing requires a certain type of *you* to be present as you engage your marketplace. While your story, your passion and your persona are critical to it, a number of additional considerations must be addressed and determined as you craft your positioning in this type of personal marketing on behalf of your business.

The goal of positioning is a compelling marketing magnetism. Your prospects are drawn to you and as a result, your business thrives.

Attraction Matters

The science of attraction is something that the world is longing to figure out. Research has been conducted for many years to determine what it really is that causes people to be attracted to one another.

A recent study conducted by Osaka University in Japan found that both men and women are attracted to someone who exhibits symmetry. This means that the person who is considered to be attractive has a face and body that mirror each other left to right. Scientists suggest that this symmetry and our reaction to it is triggered at a primitive and subconscious level. Apparently, the symmetrical person has implied health and strong genetics. Hollywood stars like Angelina Jolie, George Clooney, Jennifer Lopez, Hugh Jackman, Minka Kelly and Bradley Cooper all exhibit very obvious symmetry.

Related studies in attraction have also uncovered that it is more than biology and symmetry. It's also quite evident that there are a number of other influential factors in attraction that research continues to explore. Here are five of the most important ones.

1. **Similarity.** We like those who are like us. It's scientifically true that "birds of a feather flock together." This includes attraction to those with similar attitudes and values.
How will you display similarities with your prospects?

2. **Proximity.** We are attracted those who are physically close to us.
Can you create proximity in your marketing?
Can you find a way to be close even if your prospects are not in your backyard?

3. **Familiarity.** We like those we have frequent contact with and become familiar with. This seems related to the proximity factor above.
How are you going to create a consistent and frequent way to communicate with your prospective clients and customers?

4. **Reciprocity.** We are attracted to those who genuinely like us.
   How can you show your prospects that you like them or are concerned about their outcomes?

5. **Barriers.** We like others that we cannot have or have limited access to. While this seems to almost contradict the above listed attraction factors, it is indeed a recognized factor.
   I know from my earliest days that desire intensifies when you want something and you can't get it.
   Is there a way you can create some element of scarcity in your business such that attraction is intensified?

An understanding of how attraction works matters because the goal in a "You Are The Logo" type of marketing is to create a magnetic attraction. It seems only logical to take the science of attraction into account.

The problem with a corporate, brand-focused approach to marketing is that it fails to engage the unique human dynamic of attraction. A brand cannot "like you" so the reciprocity factor is not engaged. A brand can attempt to suggest it has similar values to you, but in reality it is inanimate. Therefore, it cannot be truly similar to you.

Attraction needs you to create the magnetic effects. Attraction and the emotional connections that derive from it are much more powerful with people than they are with brands. Engaging our prospects in a deeply personal way allows us to leverage this attraction.

Be Known. Be Liked. Be Trusted.

It has been said that people buy from those they know, like and trust. Thus, it is of critical importance to structure our marketing in such a way that we achieve these goals well in advance of ever trying to sell our services to people.

Being known, liked and trusted demands building relationships before the sale is made. It means foregoing cheap and shallow ways of doing business. Instead, we must strategize ways to ensure that we have built a reputation that precedes us.

"To be known" is more than just putting a face on an ad in a purely business sense. It means sharing your story including the good, the bad – and, yes, even the ugly parts. It's having a point of view. It's being willing to expose your exceptional qualities.

In his book, *How To Write A Damn Good Novel*, James Frey writes:

> "Readers are intrigued by characters who are good at what they do. Detectives who are extraordinary (Sherlock Holmes) are of far more interest than those who aren't. Cowboy heroes are always good at drawing a gun or tracking or some other skill. Brody in *Jaws* is extraordinarily good at being a sheriff. Quint is an extraordinarily good shark hunter."

So in order to be known, you need to share your extraordinary qualities. It is not required that this be done at a one-on-one level. It can be expressed through the marketing tactics that you employ. The amazing thing is that we have exceptional resources at our disposal that allow us to do this. Simple YouTube-style videos can help you share your story.

"To be liked" means that we have to do likeable things. Likeable people do good things for others. Being likeable is something that we express in conversation. It means we are fun and engaging. To be liked requires that we not take ourselves too seriously. Yet at the same time, we are confident and sure.

Exceptional and Flawed

Many people believe that they must be perfect in order for others to like them.

People who write fiction novels have a unique perspective on what makes a character likeable in a novel. Elizabeth George, in her book,

Write Away, suggests that real characters have flaws.

> "No one wants to read about a perfect character, so a character possessing perfection in one area should possess imperfection in another area. Sir Arthur Conan Doyle understood this, which is one of the reasons Sherlock Holmes has stood the test of time for more than 100 years. Holmes has a perfect intellect… but he's an emotional black hole incapable of sustained relationship with anyone except Dr. Watson."

Don't neglect to expose your flaws and foibles. It makes you more likeable.

When we think of Steve Jobs, we are still amazed at his vision and his passion to produce beautiful and incredible technology. Yet, he was also a flawed character as evidenced in his obsessive perfectionism and ruthless demands on his staff. Jobs was known for often being rude, dismissive, hostile and even spiteful. He was a whole person. We liked him more that way.

Oprah is a great example of someone with a willingness to expose her flaws. She is incredibly talented, but we know her very obvious struggle with her weight and her eating issues. As a public figure who has clearly strategized about how to present herself to the world, her willingness to make her body issues and her never-ending battle with her weight very public, has endeared her to us. Sharing her flaws makes her infinitely more like us. Therefore, she is more likeable.

A Mighty Theme

Trustworthiness also requires having a position. We must have a philosophy. We must stand for something.

Herman Melville, the author of *Moby Dick*, wrote:

> "To produce a mighty book, you must choose a mighty theme."

Granted, we are not writing books. However, we are exposing ourselves as the characters in our business drama. As we seek to build trust, we need a mighty theme. It must be something that we clearly stand for. Create a solid foundation for yourself, and one on which your prospects can depend. As a result, you will be more trusted.

Bill Gates wanted a "personal computer on every desk in every office, home and school" and created the software to ensure that it happened. That mighty theme created a significant amount of trust in what Gates and Microsoft were all about.

Mark Zuckerburg "wants to make the world a more open place." He is doing just that with Facebook. It's evident that almost a billion people trust him and his vision.

Warren Buffett stands for "Value Investing" and he lives that out in every investment he makes. This has provided a powerful theme with abundant success, allowing many to trust him.

Jack Welch of General Electric believed you should be "number one" or "number two" in an industry or not be in it at all. He was very public and vocal about his mighty theme. He lived it out as he ran the business. As a result, his investors and his staff trusted him.

Trust matters, especially when you elevate yourself to a major marketing role.

Putting yourself out there, not just in being known and liked, but in establishing your "big theme" tells your clients that you believe in something so much that you are willing to stake your reputation on it. From this, you earn a level of trust that is very powerful for prospective customers to see.

Your Context Influences Your Character

As you seek to establish yourself as the personality marketer for your business, the context in which you work and live becomes extremely important as to who you are perceived to be.

Dwight Swain in his book, *Creating Characters: How To Build Story People*, suggests the following.

> "Character is inextricably linked to context… separated, meaningless. Without puzzles to solve, Sherlock Holmes holds little interest. Moses unchallenged by an enslaving Egypt, Hercules without his Labors, Columbo without fascinating, intriguing, arrogant murderers would all fail to keep anyone interested in them."

As you prepare to become visible and relate your story, you need to understand that it is not only what you do – but the events and reasons surrounding it (the context) – that makes it so much more attractive to people.

I recall hearing this story from Dad. It helps to clarify this idea.

> Many years ago three men were standing by the side of the road pouring a mixture of water, sand and other ingredients into a trough. A passerby asked them what they were doing. The first said, "I am making mortar." The second answered, "I am laying bricks." However, the third proclaimed with much enthusiasm, "I am building a cathedral."

They were all doing the same thing, but the context described by the third man made the activity more interesting both to him and the passerby.

The simple things you and your company do each day become meaningful and interesting when placed in the context of the clients you serve, the complexity of the process, the role you fill in a bigger industry, and the economics associated to it. Your world, your work and your business are not boring. They are only being explained in uninteresting ways.

In my business, one of the services we offer clients is web marketing support. While web marketing appears rather simplistic to many people, in reality the idea that you can "build a website and they will come" is anything but simplistic.

Web marketing is a complex array of tasks and expertise demanding a wide range of skills and strengths. It is carried out in an environment where there is no official rulebook or suggested guidelines. We just have to figure them out. Then, when we do figure something out and create a systematic way of having the staff implement the tasks, the rules have changed by the time we begin to implement.

This is just one element of the context in which we work. When that context is explained and passed on to prospects, it creates an interest in what we do.

You have your own set of circumstances that allow you to be interesting. Thus, it is important that you talk about it and share the information.

In web marketing, we often battle the unknown.

- *In your world, what do you battle?*
- *What are the enemies that you fight and conquer?*
- *Who are the people with whom you interact?*
- *How do you help them?*
- *What are the stories of the meetings?*
- *How about the places you travel? Or where you live?*

This is an incredibly important part of the context in which your marketing character lives.

A couple of years ago, I moved from the Toronto, Ontario, Canada area to San Diego, California, U.S. This was a very significant move for me. The discussion of both locations allowed me to interact with clients and prospects in an interesting way. Even the move itself and all the related elements of the transition became part of my context.

The weather in Toronto and San Diego are very different discussions. Almost every conversation I have with people who do not live in Southern California includes some sort of discourse on how lucky I am to live here. (I always mention how close I am to the Torrey Pines Golf Course and the beach at Del Mar to ensure that the jealousy is well-established.)

In Toronto, I didn't engage the same conversations. In Toronto, conversations often began with the extremes in the weather. Snow – or the absence of it – becomes the context from which conversations commence. Context creates interest. Interest sustains relationships.

The final *context* item that you can engage in your on-going communication with clients and prospects are your personal adventures. These adventures are an important part in your continuous story.

Here are more valuable thoughts from James Frey in *How To Write A Damn Good Novel*:

> "Fictional characters – homo fictus – are not identical to flesh and blood human beings – homo sapiens. One reason for this is that readers wish to read about the exceptional rather than the mundane. Readers demand that homo fictus be more handsome or ugly, more ruthless or noble, more brave or cowardly, etc. than real people are."

As Logos for our business, we need to make sure that we walk within the boundaries of the fictional extremes. At the same time, we also need to share the parts of our lives that are bigger than ordinary life, including when we are more exceptional than just the status quo. This is why your adventures are notable as part of your context.

Mike Sullivan

Mike Sullivan is the President of Automated Records Centre in State College, Pennsylvania. While his business story and service offerings might appeal to a limited audience, Mike has an exceptional capability and talent that elevates him into someone who's bigger than ordinary. As soon as he shares this part of his story with you, it changes the context and you become interested in him.

Mike is a marathon man. Not the kind that runs one marathon at some point in life just to say he's done it. Mike has run over 30 competitive marathons so far in his life. This does not include the thousands of miles that he runs in preparation for the actual races.

So when Mike shares that exceptional part of himself and enumerates his running adventures, it is worth noting. But when he shares his story in the context of promoting his business and service offerings to a prospect, I am sure you can see how it changes the way they view him.

But I'm Not That Interesting

Oh yes, you are! Hidden in your story and in your day-to-day life, both inside-and-outside your business, there is treasure-filled wonder. You have all that you need in your life and context to create a compelling attraction. You are already capable of being known, liked and trusted. Your context gives you a place to share your wonderful personality with the world.

> There is a vitality, a life force, an energy, a quickening that is translated through you into action, and because there is only one of you in all of time, this expression is unique. And if you block it, it will never exist through any other medium and it will be lost. The world will not have it. It is not your business to determine how good it is nor how valuable nor how it compares with other expressions. It is your business to keep it yours clearly and directly, to keep the channel open.
> Martha Graham

With this uncovered, you now need to define how you will become the Logo for your business.

CHAPTER 7

You Are The Logo Design

*Create your own visual style...
let it be unique for yourself
and yet profitable for others.*
Orson Wells

There are plenty of books on how to become a personal brand. You Are The Logo has a very different focus. This is not about self-promotion as an end in itself – it is not about you obtaining all the glory. Although that might actually happen for some as a result.

You Are The Logo is about deliberately employing a proven marketing framework that will create powerful positioning for your company and, as a result, improve your business outcome.

There are various expressions or design options for engaging you as an individual in your marketing. Each expression has a different style or level of engagement.

As I have studied those who become powerful marketing personalities for their companies and businesses, these expressions and design options are my way of creating a framework to categorize the way it has been done.

For some, their expression is limited to one design option. For others, there is a definite blending of the styles. Some styles are chosen, others are evolved into. My goal in this chapter is to help you see the different ways in which you can start to engage your own style of being the Logo for your business.

The Namesake

When you think of aligning yourself and your business, one of the easiest ways to do this is to simply name your company after yourself. While not sexy – if you want to run a business that leverages you – naming the company after yourself is a powerful marketing tool.

When you think of many of the luxury items in the world, you'll be surprised at how many of them are actually the namesake of the founder of the business.

Donna Karan, Ralph Lauren, Tory Burch, Calvin Klein, Kate Spade, Michael Kors, Vera Wang and Armani are all elite fashion brands named for their founder. Dom Perignon is named after the Benedictine Monk who was an important quality pioneer for Champagne. Bentley, Rolls Royce, Ferrari, Bugatti and Lamborghini are all automobile companies named after the original founders. Bang and Olufsen, as well as Harmon/Kardon are well known audio brand names of their respective founding partners. Carl Zeiss is the world renowned camera lens. Dyson makes exceptional vacuums. Bausch and Lomb are leaders in the optical world.

I could go on and on. All these premium and exclusive companies are named after their founders.

When your name is on the door, there is an immediate tie to you and to a personal, premium boutique-style commitment from you as the owner and founder.

I recognize that you might already have a business name, so changing your business name to be your own may not be realistic or appropriate. However, if you are contemplating launching a new company and want to be a premium provider, consider being the namesake for your company. It's a proven model to connect the owner to the business.

The Spokesperson

A primary spokesperson is the most recognizable expression to establish yourself as the Logo for your business.

Essentially, in this strategy the owner or executive becomes the primary marketing and advertising spokesperson for the company. This means showing up in some, most, or even all of the advertising that a company produces.

Advertising in a local business environment for many means radio, TV and newspaper – especially when the audience is a consumer. In more diverse settings it could take other forms including online video, direct mail or niche-focused media advertising.

It is in these advertising settings that the owner or executive is pictured, recorded or videotaped delivering the message and is essential to the actual advertisement.

In many cases, these ads incorporate some different variations:

- The spokesperson introduces the company
- The spokesperson introduces a service or product
- The spokesperson delivers a special offer

Jerry Navarra

Jerry Navarra is the President of Jerome's Furniture in San Diego, California. Jerry appears in almost all of the advertising his company does on radio, TV and the newspaper.

He built his stores on the philosophy of "no glitter," a phrase meant to explain the company's discounted prices through low overhead warehouse displays. In all his ads, he represents the philosophy. Jerry is down to earth, without any big over-the-top antics.

In the broadcast media ads, Jerry is talking about new furniture, or a special deal he's having in his stores, or explaining a reason you should visit his stores. In print ads, his picture is present with the furniture specials depicted. These ads support the personal connection that he has built as the face of the company. When you arrive at the website, Jerry is visibly present. In fact, at the time of writing this book, Jerry anchors the website on every single page.

Tom Dickson

Tom Dickson is a name you might not recognize, but he is a primary spokesperson sensation. Tom Dickson founded Blendtec – a company that produces a line of blenders, mills and mixers.

In late 2006, Tom launched Blentec's first infomercial on YouTube. It generated amazing results. This led to a YouTube series entitled, *"Will It Blend?"* in which he routinely blends all manner of items from golf balls to cubic zirconia to skeletons (and more recently an iPhone and an iPad).

What makes his series so fun is that it will often be connected to something in the news or "pop culture." Tom has been the spokesperson on this web video series, which has had incredible viral success.

Interestingly, this is the only place Tom shows up as spokesperson. He is not listed on their website or other product related advertising. Thus, he has a very defined spokesperson marketing role.

Frank Buckley

Buckley's is a Canadian medicinal company that makes a signature product called *Buckley's Mixture*. It's a unique combination of Camphor, Menthol, Canadian Balsam, Pine Needle Oil and Tincture of Capsicum.

Their tagline for the product is: "It tastes awful. And it works."

Frank Buckley started this brutally honest campaign about their hard-to-swallow medicine when he became President of the company in the mid-80's. Frank took on the role of spokesperson to explain that he didn't like the terrible taste of *Buckley's Mixture* either. "But it worked!"

It was a brilliant strategy of selling a product while relating to the public on a personal level. It was the best role Frank Buckley could have taken as the company's president.

The spokesperson role is one you can easily step into. Leveraging all the factors discussed in the previous chapters, the role of the spokesperson for your business is something that will be incredibly valuable to try, even if only on a trial basis.

The Expert

An explicit expert is the noted and recognized knowledge leader in a certain area, discipline or field. This might only be noticeable to a very small group of clients or prospects. The expertise could also extend to an entire industry. This strategy generally demands that you use the knowledge you have gained or compiled. Then, as an expert,

> *If you are going to be the obvious expert, you need to have a body of work.*
> Doug Hall

you deliver this knowledge as the front end of your marketing funnel. In many cases, this education is the magnetic device to bring prospects to you. By providing them with an education, you are perceived as the authority.

There is a wealth of potential ways to deliver educational marketing. You can deliver speeches, special workshops, or even webinars. You could write to support this educational focus delivered in formats like a blog, a special report, an article – or even a book.

The goal is to educate your prospects. Positioning yourself as the expert in any business context seems logical, but you'd be surprised at how few actually do it.

Matt Mullenweg

Matt Mullenweg has established himself as the leading expert on the blogging and content management system platform, WordPress. This was not particularly difficult since he actually was its founding developer. With WordPress serving more than 15% of all sites on the Internet today, Matt is well established as the global expert on its most important website development platform.

As the software itself is open source, Matt isn't using his expertise to sell the actual software, but he is definitely a passionate advocate of it. He understands the entire WordPress ecosystem and speaks regularly about where the software development is currently and where it is going.

Matt's role as the leading WordPress expert supports his profit producing business, Automattic – which provides an array of WordPress tools and resources as well as fee-based hosting of WordPress sites, WordPress security, backups and more.

There are numerous other companies that provide the exact same type of services. However, as the expert, Matt's presence attracts many to the Automattic service offerings. Not surprisingly, his paid hosting, security and backup solutions are all premium-priced products. Expert status brings premium results.

Along with being the spokesperson for your business, taking the role of expert is a very logical expression and highly effective way to position yourself as the market authority. This will assuredly attract business. Simply start to find ways to teach before you sell. It can and will make a significant impact.

The Philanthropist

A philanthropist is often seen as one who gives money for the good of society. Philanthropy has also been described as private initiatives for public good. For years, business individuals have contributed to their communities in ways that are not reimbursed. This means investing their time, expertise, money and resources to support all manner of public good. This constitutes my definition of philanthropy.

While a less overt expression of a marketing Logo, this particular style might be one of the most quietly potent ways to build a definitive reputation and positioning in a local marketplace, business community or larger industry. The willingness to get involved and contribute is the hallmark of philanthropy.

Lori Palmer

Lori Palmer is the Executive Vice President for REB Storage Systems International of Chicago, Illinois. REB specializes in engineering, consolidating and installing racking systems for the commercial records storage industry. Lori has created a powerful Logo position in the industry due to her philanthropy.

She is a tireless contributor to the industry in so many ways. She is a sponsor of every event the industry association creates as well as many of the peripheral organizations and events within the industry. Lori sits on the board of directors for the international association.

Many would pat themselves on the back and feel good about just doing this. However, Lori gives even more. Having attended many conferences and observed her in action, she never misses an opportunity to give back to her clients. She always has a full dinner slate with not just one client, but usually many. Her noted philanthropy within the industry has elevated her to a place where she magnetically attracts prospects to her. Lori gets business that nobody else even bids on simply because of her reputation.

It's Not Just About Giving Money

If you don't have dollars to give, you have many other things that are valuable to your community. Your time, your resources and your expertise can support your prospect community or industry.

Scott McNelley

Scott McNelley owns a full-service moving company in Montgomery, Alabama. He's not the largest mover in town, but he has created a local reputation for himself by giving what he has to support a diverse set of needs in his town.

He is involved in the leadership of many local service groups and business associations. Scott contributes the use of his moving trucks as the need arises. He makes room in his warehouses for events.

Through all this, Scott builds a reputation that is respected and appreciated through his community. As a result, he gets opportunities to bid on and win business based on the relationships developed in the context of his philanthropic service.

Philanthropy is an expression of abundance. Abundance is attractive. While the goal of giving to your community, industry or world is not to get a reward, somehow the universe rewards those who are generous with more.

The Celebrity

This style of marketing leverages one of two concepts. You either:

1. Bring existing celebrity status from the outside to elevate your business and make it more attractive by virtue of your popularity; or

2. You use your business as the platform to elevate your celebrity.

Celebrity is a powerful force for attraction. As discussed in an earlier chapter, people follow and respond to celebrity. Celebrity ownership of a business essentially creates a "halo effect" which helps to create press coverage, interviews and investment to the business.

Celebrity Salad Dressing

Picture yourself walking into a supermarket and heading down the salad dressing aisle. As you survey the huge selection of salad dressings, your eyes are inevitably drawn to the Newman's Own brand. The celebrity connection makes the dressing infinitely more appealing than if it was just called Newman's and had no apparent connection to actor Paul Newman himself. With relatively limited shelf space and premium pricing, Newman's Own is considered one of the top premium food companies in the world.

The connection of celebrity to products is a proven marketing model – but it extends to more than just products.

A General Store

It's not easy to elevate a general store to anything more than that, but with a celebrity owner involved, things change.

The Marshfield Hills General Store is owned by Steve Carell, the actor best known for his role on *The Office*. This store in the quiet town of Marshfield, just south of Boston, was purchased and refurbished by Steve and his family. His sister runs the store, but Steve's ownership of the store gives it an unfair advantage in terms of its attractiveness to those who shop there.

The list of celebrities who own businesses are relatively well known. Some examples include: Ashton Kutcher and his new media company, Katalyst Media; Gwen Stefani's LAMB clothing line; Sammy Hagar's Cabo Wabo Tequila Company; Olivia Newton John's Gaia Retreat and Spa; George Foreman's grills; Jessica Simpson's clothing and shoe line and John Elway's car dealerships. And the list goes on.

I recognize that you may not be in that category. You are not a celebrity, yet. Don't write it off. Don't automatically assume this expression of You Are The Logo marketing is not for you.

Microcelebrity

Celebrity does not always mean "world-famous." It might just mean famous to a select group of people – it might mean famous within an industry or within a community. In many cases, the celebrity comes as a result of the work you do in the industry or community.

If I mentioned that I had some interesting ideas from someone named Rand Fishkin, you probably wouldn't care. However, if I said the same name to a bunch of SEO business owners, they'd stop what they were doing and take note. In the traditional business world, the name means nothing, but in the SEO world, Rand is a big-time celebrity. He has developed one of the most powerful Search Engine Optimization software tools, and is a highly respected leader in the industry. He has leveraged the power of longevity in the industry, expert status and enough spokesperson appearances to have elevated himself to celebrity status.

> Microcelebrity is the phenomenon of being extremely well-known not to millions but to a small group – a thousand people, or maybe a few dozen. As DIY Media reach ever deeper into our lives, it's happening to more and more of us.
> Clive Thomson

Marsha Collier is also in those ranks. She is a celebrity in the eBay world. Perry Marshall is a celebrity in the Google AdWords industry. Mari Smith is a celebrity in the Facebook world. Craig Proctor is a celebrity in the real estate industry and Ron Ipach is a celebrity in the auto repair industry. None of these people have a TV or sports pedigree. They are front-and-center in the marketing of their businesses – and as a result derive the benefits of celebrity – without the hassles of the paparazzi.

Their fame has not been an instant thing. These microcelebrities have worked hard to create and sustain a level of celebrity as a result of their businesses. This can be the case when you leverage your spokesperson status over the years, or when your expertise creates a situation where you become elevated above simple expert status.

Mel Lastman

Mel Lastman started in the used furniture business at just 22 years of age. This was back in 1955 in Toronto. He called his store Bad Boy Furniture and, with some success, grew it to a small chain of stores in the greater Toronto area. Mel was a master at marketing. He loved publicity stunts and is well known for traveling to the Arctic in the 1960's to sell a refrigerator to an Eskimo. That stunt provided a level of celebrity that exceeded the one he had garnered as the company spokesperson.

He eventually sold the Bad Boy stores and ran for public office. Mel became the Mayor of North York, a suburb of Toronto, and ultimately was elected the Mayor of Toronto.

During his term as Mayor, his son and another partner revived his Bad Boy stores. After his term had ended, he was back in the spotlight "bigger and badder" than ever. Mel has leveraged the celebrity he garnered as Mayor to further establish his presence as a business celebrity.

Lynn Winter

Lynn Winter started as a custom woodworker and loved to incorporate art into everyday life. A twist of fate led her to wait tables which inspired her to get into the restaurant business. In 1991, Lynn opened the Paradise Café in Louisville, Kentucky. It's not only a tribute to her originality but also a unique and colorful café that introduces new twists on food and drinks.

As her restaurant soared in local popularity, so did her reputation in the food industry. This success built her greater celebrity status. Lynn has won awards and been profiled on many prominent TV shows. Now, her café has become even more popular.

Celebrity doesn't come unexpectedly. It is the reward to those who are willing to embrace the very public role that celebrity status requires. You have to be out there. You have to be visible. You have to be different. You have to be good at what you do. When all of that provides a small level of celebrity – the rewards for the business are very tangible.

The Icon

An established icon is someone who has risen to a level of prominence in both their business and their industry. For many, the iconic status has never been a priority or a hallmark of their style. Often their company or their product gets a level of exposure in the marketplace – and as the CEO or founder – they are thrust into a very public role.

Others who have reached this particular status have been more overt in their attempt to be the face of their business. In either case, these iconic leaders don't downplay their role. They embrace it to their company's advantage. They use the opportunities presented to them by virtue of their role and assert themselves as the public face of the business.

Richard Branson

Richard Branson is one of the best examples of the established icon. He *is* Virgin, but is not the primary advertising spokesperson for any of the various 400 Virgin Group entities in their everyday commercials. He does, however, have a larger than life presence as the face and personality for the entire Virgin enterprise.

Over the years his willingness to do incredible, even outrageous things – such as the Atlantic crossings in boats and in hot air balloons – has elevated his iconic status, and, as a result, the Virgin brand. He continues to create continual exposure for himself and Virgin with his exploratory adventures into space and undersea.

Branson has willingly stepped into the spotlight. He has appeared on TV for years as an interviewee, and has even tried his own TV series similar to Donald Trump's *The Apprentice*. Branson remains involved in large, global humanitarian causes.

His name, reputation and business savvy as the corporate icon behind the Virgin business makes him the most obvious example of this concept.

Other Icons

Steve Jobs also played this role. He was not the featured spokesperson, but he was the iconic leader of the business. Anita Roddick of The Body Shop did as well. Jack Welch of GE and Michael Dell of Dell all fit this role. Meg Whitman of HP also lives in this category. The list of these types of icons is pretty substantial.

> Everything a CEO says and does is no longer personal. It is attributed to the company.
> Shelly Lazarus

Bill Gates at Microsoft, Mark Zuckerburg at Facebook, and Jeff Bezos at Amazon are all very visible as the iconic person or personality of their companies – but don't necessarily play the role of the advertising spokesperson.

This "established icon" expression of You Are The Logo marketing seems to work best when there is a lot of interest in the business already. It is not likely to be the default approach for companies with little or no press. If you are just starting out, or are trying to grow from a small company to a mid-sized company, I'd encourage you to first focus on the spokesperson, expert or philanthropist roles to get started. That being said, I encourage you to "Think Big!"

What is very evident to me in the role the established icons play is the almost fanatical preparation for the big events.

Steve Jobs could launch a product like no other. Mark Zuckerburg has a definite opinion about how the business should operate and displays that clearly when he is on stage or in interviews. Meg Whitman is incredibly effective at dealing with the political minefields in communicating with business media.

When the big moments come, these established icons show up – *prepared*.

Logo Style Crossover

Many of the Logos outlined in this book express themselves in more than one of the style categories. As they crossover between the various expressions, their authority and respect increases.

The optimal approach for you is to find a way to incorporate all of the elements into your marketing.

As the namesake, it may not be possible to name your business after yourself. However, you might be able to create an exclusive service category or personal guarantee named after yourself.

> If you don't get noticed, you don't have anything. You just have to be noticed, but the art is in getting noticed naturally, without screaming or without tricks.
> Leo Burnett

As the spokesperson, you point people to your business and company by announcing your products and services.

As the expert, you teach prospects and clients important information. You provide the context from which they make intelligent decisions. In addition, you use your expertise to position yourself against the pack.

As a philanthropist, you are seen as a leading contributor to your community. You give not only charitably but also because it serves your community or constituency. Though not expected, the inevitable reward is that you are respected.

As a celebrity, you are trying to create a following of those who just want to be part of your world. You need to bring charisma and a story to what you do. You can't afford to be boring.

As an icon, when you get the chances you act on them by seizing the moment, even if the world doesn't see it yet. You show stability, wisdom, character and balanced perspective. You have established yourself and your business.

With this simple framework of styles, you have some definite ways to express your personality on behalf of your business. You might choose to stick solidly to one style or develop your own unique crossover styles.

However, a style choice is not enough. You have to *do* something and act on it.

The second half of this book outlines a complete array of specific tactics you can engage to support becoming the Logo for your business.

SECTION 2

How To Implement You Are The Logo Marketing

If you are not willing to risk the usual you will have to settle for the ordinary.
Jim Rohn

CHAPTER 8

A Logo Speaks

According to most studies, people's number one fear is public speaking. Number two is death. Death is number two. Does that sound right? This means to the average person, if you go to a funeral, you're better off in the casket than doing the eulogy.
Jerry Seinfeld

Without question, most of the people who create personal name recognition and serve as the Logo for their business leverage the power of public speaking to their advantage. In my opinion, this is one of the most powerful tools to place in your arsenal of tactics as the Logo for your business.

My First Speech

My 6th grade speech for student council at Oxbow Public School was a seminal moment in my life. I can remember it to this day. Those feelings I experienced that day so many years ago still linger in my mind every time I think about speaking in a public setting.

As an observer for a number of years through my early grades, I recall watching the speeches by the senior student hopefuls. The pattern was pretty similar. It went something like this… Walk to the front of the gymnasium once your name was called. Pull out the index cards and tentatively tell the students assembled on the gymnasium floor in front of you how you want to do some amazing thing such as demand better lunch snacks, or more fun intramural activities.

When I decided that I wanted to be on the student council, I realized that I needed to do it differently. My goal was to do something that would cause the entire student body to vote without having to actually think about the decision. I wanted to do a speech that would make it impossible for them *not* to vote for me. I was not willing to deliver anything less than the best speech ever given at Oxbow.

So, I abandoned recipe cards in favor of something I thought was better suited to a political speech. I used toilet paper. For the record, I wanted to run a "clean campaign."

I didn't walk to the front of the gym when my name was called like the others. I stood from my spot three quarters of the way back in the gym and began my speech by clearly and distinctly delivering my opening sentence. Then I unrolled my toilet paper notes as I slowly – and deliberately delivered my speech standing among my peers.

By the time I finished, I had moved to the front of the gymnasium and everyone in my entire school (even the ultra cool 8th graders!) and the teachers were on their feet applauding. Standing ovations are hard to get in 6th grade during election speeches, but I did it.

It was a moment of pure joy. It was even more important than winning the election to represent the 6th grade class on the Oxbow Public School Student Council. That speech became the foundation and birthplace of more student council speeches and subsequent victories in the years to come.

In University, I actually sang my student council speech while I sat at the grand piano on the stage. So, speeches have worked for me.

Yet it wasn't in school where I discovered the potent effects of speaking in a public setting – it was in business. That's where the more significant impact has been felt in my own history.

Along with my own personal experiences and in my extensive research into personal Logo style marketing, it is quite clear that the willingness and ability to speak publicly is a great way to launch, improve or solidify a position and reputation in an industry or in a community.

There is something that happens when you stand to deliver a speech. You stand apart from the listeners and, in the act of providing them with knowledge, information, advice and story, the audience gives you their respect – and in many cases, their business.

Feel the Fear and Do It Anyway

For most people, speaking in public is a greatly feared activity, especially for those who don't enjoy being in front of an audience. However, for those who do choose to engage it for themselves, the results are dramatic.

If you do fear speaking in public, an important way to conquer your fear is simply to practice – a lot. Hundreds of thousands of business leaders around the world have benefited from getting involved in communication and leadership organizations such as Toastmasters International, and, as a result, have learned to craft and present simple to eloquent speeches. You don't get better by studying speeches; you get better by giving them. Toastmasters Clubs provide a supportive environment to practice your way to a better business.

Speeches Work

If you doubt the incredible power of speeches, then look at what has happened in the TED community. TED – Technology, Entertainment,

Design – is an invitation-only conference held annually in California where some of the world's most fascinating thinkers and doers come to speak. Speakers are challenged to give the talk of their lives in just 18 minutes or less.

Chris Anderson, the curator of TED, founded the organization as a nonprofit whose goal was to foster the spread of great ideas. The TED conference has morphed into hundreds of conferences around the world all wrapped around the 18-minute speech. The videos of those speeches have been viewed over 500 million times online and that number grows rapidly every day.

Speeches work. Every day across the business world, groups get together to listen to people speak within the context of business. CEOs speak to shareholders of the Fortune 1000 elite businesses. These speeches determine stock prices as well as the confidence of their investors. CEOs also speak to their staff and to their markets. Steve Jobs was a master of these speaking events, especially as he launched new products to the Apple faithful.

Speeches to your niche audience are one of the best ways to position yourself as an expert in your category. They allow you to not only show your knowledge and expertise – but they also allow you to exhibit your personality and share your story.

Book An Engagement. Sell It Before You Develop It

You can work to hammer out a speech. You can practice. You can revise it. You can repeat the process again and again to get it to where you're ready to speak in front of people. However, if you gave a speech and no one came, how discouraging would that be?

You can believe that speaking will help your business, but if you never speak, it won't make any difference. Book a speaking engagement and then craft your speech. Every single business and service organization in your city needs a speaker. There are Rotary Clubs, Optimists Clubs, Chamber of Commerce meetings, as well as a myriad of industry or market groups where you can speak. To build your confidence and get some practice, speak to the smallest one you can find.

Your speech doesn't have to be perfect. Having a deadline is going to get you motivated to actually prepare your speech. Ask any reporter, there's nothing like a deadline to get you to crank out your best work.

Speech Development

The preparation ritual for developing a speech is different for every person. If you are creating a "stump" speech – the kind that you'll deliver time and time again to different audiences like politicians running for office – you spend a lot of time crafting every part of it. But if you are developing a "one and done" speech to an industry conference or local service group, it's more important to work mostly on the main points and the general flow.

Some people are comfortable structuring their notes in a way that allows them to speak in a more impromptu manner using a list of main points and bullets. Others prefer to write their entire speech out word-for-word. Some like to deliver speeches that are highly prepared but allows them to ad-lib and improvise as necessary.

It usually takes more than three weeks to prepare a good impromptu speech.
Mark Twain

Even though this is not a book on how to create a speech, I do have some important ideas for you to bring to every speech you develop.

Initially, I would encourage you to have a BIG idea.

- What's the point of your presentation – your main objective?
- What are you trying to get them to know, learn, change or think?

This leads to the second big area of preparation.

- Who are they?
- Where is your audience in relation to your big idea?
- What's at stake if they don't adopt your big idea?

- Once you've finished your speech, where do you want them to be?

Armed with that foundational knowledge, build a speech that helps them to get there. Use stories to connect emotionally. Use logic to support your big idea. Give them an understanding of where they are now and where they could be.

Your goal in any type of public speaking opportunity is to leave your audience with something of value. So once you've developed your speech, go out and make it happen.

Broadcast Speeches

With the advent of easy ways to record yourself and place what you create online, I encourage you to start creating mini-speeches. Don't record yourself standing in the front of a room acting like you are speaking to a seated audience. Videotape yourself giving a short speech to the audience on the other side of your camera lens. Take a topic you are passionate about and draft a simple outline. Then video record yourself and put it on YouTube.

Get yourself out there, even if it is only on YouTube. You might not become the Justin Beiber of the speaking world with a few short videos online, but you will gain some confidence.

Teach a Live Class, Seminar or Workshop

An even better way to create expert positioning in your business may be by teaching a class or hosting a workshop.

Sarah "Bogi" Lateiner runs a company called 180° Automotive in Phoenix, Arizona. Through a unique workshop, Sarah teaches women (and some men) how to maintain their car. Her mission is to inform women, through these educational opportunities, to take an active role in caring for their vehicles. As you may have guessed, she is in demand as a mechanic for the services she offers. The workshops build her credibility.

Whatever business or service you are in, you can teach your prospects something. As a provider of a service, there are things you know that your clients don't. There are mistakes they make or opportunities they miss that you could help them with.

While a speech might not be the best place to do this, a seminar, workshop or class can provide a unique opportunity to not only give your prospects some much needed knowledge – it will also provide you with powerful positioning and a reputation that supports your marketing and sales.

Offer live workshops, but don't forget you can do them online or virtually as well. Webinars and teleseminars are excellent ways to make the workshop experience more accessible for people anytime, anywhere. Even if your prospects are all in your backyard, webinars allow them to learn without leaving their offices or their homes.

Let Us March

There is a famous story from Greek history about two statesmen and orators, Pericles and Demosthenes. It is written of them that after they delivered their speeches, the people would respond. In response to Pericles they would say "What a great speaker! Yet, in response to Demosthenes they would say, "Let us march!"

Your goal for every speech is to have your audience want to *act*, to *change*… to do *something*… to *march*.

Sam Seaborn, fictional Deputy White House Communications Director on the TV show *The West Wing*, once said this while discussing a speech:

> "The difference between a good speech and a great speech is the energy with which the audience comes to their feet at the end. Is it polite? Is it a chore? Are they standing up because

> their boss just stood up? No. We want it to come from their socks."

My hope for you is that, after your listeners hear your speech, they respond from their socks. As a result, you will be someone they respect and admire. Speeches can change your business world as they have mine. I encourage you to speak as the Logo for your business.

CHAPTER 9

A Logo Writes

The reason one writes isn't the fact he wants to say something.
He writes because he has something to say.
F. Scott Fitzgerald

If you wish to position yourself as an authority – or expert in any business or field – writing can be an extremely powerful way to raise your profile and credibility. These include articles, columns, special reports, tip books, white papers, email autoresponders or a book.

Write Articles

We think of an article as a traditional news report or story written by a reporter or professional writer. However, the Internet has created a new type of article, one where you don't have to be a paid desk reporter to get published. You can do it on your own website.

Traditionally called blogging, this is nothing more than posting articles you write for your prospects or target audience to read. Simply add these to your own website blog or find a website that reaches your target audience and ask the editor or owner if you can submit an article on a particular topic.

You can definitely write for print publications, as there are plenty of opportunities to do so. They are always looking for valuable content. Depending on your niche, there are most likely specialty or trade publications for your audience. These can be great outlets for you to provide articles that teach or advise, while at the same time, solidifying your positioning as the expert.

An article typically lays out the facts surrounding an issue. You can interview experts on a specific topic in person or over the phone. Later you rely on text and web sources to provide background for your article.

One extremely successful article writing strategy is to conduct "Question & Answer" interviews. These can be with other professionals in your industry or simply people with a perspective on an issue that you think your clients and prospective businesses would be interested in learning more about.

Write Columns

Columns are effective because you are the voice that is expressing an opinion. Many newspapers and magazines allow people to submit guest columns, often called "opinion-editorials" or "op-eds." If they agree to publish your column, it will occasionally be with your photo next to the byline.

Norm Brodsky

Norm Brodsky, founder of CitiStorage in New York City, New York, is a successful entrepreneur who leveraged writing to create a significant name for himself. Norm's reputation not only transcended his company but also supported it. He reached a broader audience and gained more visibility in the business world through writing a column in *Inc.* Magazine called "Street Smarts."

Along with a number of books co-authored with Bo Burlingham, Norm has been doing the column in *Inc.* since 1995. Until he sold the business in 2008, Norm used his monthly column to educate his readers about all elements of his business and what he was learning along the way. Now he teaches readers about his new business adventures in hotel building.

In writing these monthly columns, Norm significantly enhanced his reputation and standing in the international business community. This no doubt had a significant effect on the credibility and prestige he automatically brought to each business meeting with potential prospects and clients.

Magazines and specialty publications need regular contributors similar to what Norm Brodsky provides for *Inc.* Magazine. If you have an audience that reads a specific local or industry publication, then a regular column can be a strong way to position yourself.

The key to great columns is to have a strong opinion. Readers won't respond to a bland, middle of the road, "shoulder-shrug" column. They want something bold. Don't be afraid to express how you really feel, but be sure to back it up with facts.

Write Special Reports

Do you ever watch TV shows such as *Frontline* or *60 Minutes*? These programs epitomize the "special report," which is an in-depth look at a particular issue.

Conduct a Google search for "special report" and you'll find that every publication from *The Economist* to *Reuters* has a section devoted to thorough articles on timely issues. Being *timely* is the key to a successful special report; if it's not a pertinent issue then your prospects won't be interested.

These reports don't have to be lengthy investigative pieces. They can be concise and still shed light on an issue that your readers had no idea about.

Your report should also have some connection to your professional expertise. It can be a great way to tell prospective clients, "I don't think you know about 'x,' so I am going to show you why it matters and what you can do about it."

Rich Schefren is business management guru to the Internet marketing industry. A number of years ago, he wrote a special report titled, *Internet Business Manifesto*. It outlined how those who seek to have an online business are struggling. Rich addresses how to solve it in his manifesto. That single report has been downloaded more than a million times. Those reports have led to even more reports which fuel the front end of his business marketing funnel.

Write Tip Books

A tip book is a multi-page booklet or pamphlet that focuses on providing helpful information and tips on a specific topic relevant to your prospects. The topic is always something you are the expert on for your niche.

The Nine Inside Secrets You Must Know to Slash Your Premiums.

How to Pay for Your Alternative Health Care with Tax-Free Dollar$-- AND Financially Survive a Medical Disaster!

These titles are simple and easy tip books created by Victoria Eden, an independent insurance advisor in Acworth, Georgia. She's been called the "insurance marketing queen."

Use your expertise and special perspective in your field to develop your tip book. Share your "secrets" and unique strategies, but share them in a simple format – numbered or bulleted – not report format.

When readers feel confident they are gaining knowledge they can't get anywhere else, they'll return to you as a trusted source of information.

Write White Papers

White papers have become the bread and butter of many people in the marketing world, especially in business-to-business marketing communication.

They started out as guides to help government officials make decisions about policy. In many cases, a white paper was the document that was the actual explanation of a government policy.

By definition, a white paper is an authoritative report or guide that helps solve a problem – more specifically, it is how *you* would solve a problem. White papers make a case for why clients should chose you, your products, methods, philosophy, technology and other tools you possess to solve a problem.

While similar in some ways to a report, white papers tend to be seen as the meatiest of written documents. If you have a highly technical prospect base and wish to elevate your position to that of an expert, publishing and distributing a white paper is much more respected than delivering a special report.

The key to success is to pick a specific problem, explain what it is and why it matters to your readers. Then, lay out your solution and explain what makes you different in solving it.

Write Emails

One more powerful tool in your writing arsenal is a structured, consistent, predetermined sequence of written emails that are automatically sent in response to someone providing you with their email address. These are often called autoresponders because the emails are sent automatically in response to a subscription.

If you do any kind of marketing online for your business, autoresponders allow you to write a series of follow-up emails in advance. Once triggered by a visitor opt-in, autoresponders can continue to work for you after someone has given you their email address.

Online marketers have tested the performance of autoresponders as compared to simple sales pages and the results are pretty astounding. Jonathan Mizel, most famous for being the editor of the *Online Marketing Letter*, once said that every message he adds to his auto-responder series brings him a $10,000 yearly raise.

Perry Marshall and Bryan Todd, the authors of *The Definitive Guide to Google AdWords*, did an experiment to compare the actual sales results of a 50/50 split test. They drove online visitors either to a sales landing page only *or* to an auto-responder opt-in page. From the opt-in page, once the visitor subscribed, they received a daily sequence of emails offering small bites of the content and then encouraged them to go back to the same sales page.

By the eighth day of their experiment, the autoresponder test group out-purchased the simple sales letter group by 91%. Perry Marshall was quick to point out that this 91% difference was only measured to the eighth day of the experiment. Imagine the impact of weeks, months and even years of an autoresponder working to re-market, teach or educate your prospective clients?

Dr. Glen Livingston is a well-respected Clinical Psychologist with specialty expertise in marketing, market research and psychological theories. He is well-known for his work in determining hyper-responsive buyers and how to get them to respond to sales offers. He's also a business owner who is the Logo for his business. Regarding his own automated email marketing, Dr. Glen states, "If a guy's been getting great content from me for two years, he feels as though he knows me; then suddenly him paying me $1,000 an hour for a phone consultation is no problem."

The key to sequential, automated email marketing is that your emails must be worthwhile and interesting. If your emails are boring and dull, they get dumped into the junk folder with every other similar email. If all you do is sell, you will quickly get relegated to spam.

However, if you can deliver emails that people willingly want to open and read, then you are in a very powerful position to generate results for your business.

Write A Traditional Book

This is the mother lode… the Holy Grail of writing. To write an *entire book* may seem like an impossible feat, but think of the exposure authors receive when they publish one.

Authors get asked to speak. They're invited on the talk show circuit. They get radio interviews, magazine profiles and reviews in the newspapers. Books create buzz, no doubt about it.

Books imply that the writer is an expert and therefore is highly credible. Books also elevate people to unique status as a published author – and microcelebrity.

Martha Stewart has written dozens of books. Richard Branson wrote *Losing My Virginity*; Charlene Lee wrote *Groundswell*; Sam Walton, *Made in America*; Gary Vaynerchuk, *Crush It!*; Jillian Michaels, *Unlimited*; Norm Brodsky and Bo Burlingham, *The Knack*; Harvey Mackay, *Swim With The Sharks*; Tony Hsieh, *Delivering Happiness*; Jason Fried, *ReWork*; and Gary Hirshberg, *Stirring It Up*.

> I went for years not finishing anything. Because, of course, when you finish something you can be judged… I had poems which were re-written so many times I suspect it was just a way of avoiding sending them out.
> Erica Jong

The goal of You Are The Logo marketing is to create a powerful positioning and a definitive reputation that will attract people – and a published book will certainly help do the trick!

You as the Scribe

From these examples you can see that there are many avenues you can take with writing. There's no limit to the types of pieces you can write or the publications in which you can be featured.

Writing is one of the most effective ways to reach a broader audience. As I've described in previous chapters, it's not the only way, but it certainly helps to create that ubiquitous presence you're going for.

Once you've got your writing going, keep it up! Otherwise, you'll disappear into the background. Even if you move more towards emphasizing speaking engagements or TV appearances, keep on writing. Keep putting new information out there. It's the snowball effect. The more you write, the bigger your presence is going to get.

CHAPTER 10

A Logo Writes Repeatedly

Exercise the writing muscle every day, even if it is only a letter, notes, a title list, a character sketch, a journal entry. Writers are like dancers, like athletes. Without that exercise, the muscles seize up.
Jane Yolen

This chapter describes a critically important writing tactic and one that allows consistency in establishing a position within your marketplace.

As I've suggested before, you need to think in terms of campaign-oriented marketing. You cannot just do something once. The requirement is to market, then "rinse and repeat." You need to view marketing as a never completed goal that demands consistency and persistence.

Newsletters

Newsletters give you the opportunity to do that. When you communicate repetitively, you cement your presence with your prospective clients and constituency.

A newsletter has a few key characteristics:

- It is a *regular* publication. If you only send one item in the mail or via email, and then never do it again, it's not a newsletter.
- A newsletter is a way to communicate your expertise and positioning while establishing a relationship with your readers.
- Everything from the main subject of the newsletter to the specific content you write has to have some value to your readers.

If your newsletter has no pertinence to their lives – if it doesn't offer them a valuable piece of advice or the latest industry news they want to hear about – there's no reason for them to read it. Your goal is to have them *want* to receive it.

By their very nature, newsletters establish you as the expert. They solidify your presence because they are consistent. Your readers are going to come to expect and eagerly await your newsletters the second they're finished reading the current one.

Think "Enquirer" Not Just "Industry Insider"

"Zany Holidays," "The Random Fact File" and "Holiday Trivia, Amusing Stories."

You'd have no idea these column headlines belonged to an insurance newsletter, would you? These are pulled right from Victoria Eden and her *Victoria's View* monthly newsletter.

She also has columns that include information like "Be a Better Buyer," "Insurance Word of the Month," and "Freebie of the Month."

Look at a copy of the *National Enquirer* magazine and you see titles like, "Runway Star Arrested Over Cat Fight!" and "Don't Get in a Knife Fight with the Clintons!"

These titles are sensationalized and totally over the top, but completely entertaining to read. Headlines and titles sell magazines.

Of course, you'll be giving insider tips to your newsletter readers – information that is beneficial and that can't be found anywhere else – but in order to get them to read what you wrote, you must use titles that will catch their interest.

Give Them Good News

Your newsletters are going to be positive. They are going to be affirming. They are going to be empowering with headlines such as:

"You can save money!"

"You can buy a home!"

"You can make your retirement dreams come true!"

When you are upbeat and positive in your messages, you're going to gain a loyal following of newsletter readers. Even if you are writing about negative things – subjects like fraud, accident rates or divorce – you can make your message positive with headlines such as:

"Let me show you how you can avoid these traps and walk away with more cash in your pocket."

"How to Spot the 'Bad Guys' a Mile Away."

Offer your readers something they don't get everyday… good news!

Rub Your Personality All Over It

If I handed you two newsletters, asked you to study them for five minutes, then held them up in front of you and asked, "Who wrote the one on the left and who wrote the one on the right?" the answers should jump out of your mouth.

Bill Glazer tells business people, "Be outrageous in your mailing materials. Stand out from the pile. Don't blend in with the junk mail."

Put yourself into your newsletter. *Make it the paper version of your actual personality*. Readers will recognize it just as readily as if they saw you walking down the street.

Your readers won't just recognize your newsletter, they'll also know exactly what lies in store for them when they start to read it. They'll know what kind of advice you'll offer, what kind of jokes you'll throw in there, and what kind of stories you'll tell.

Always be sure to include your picture. Readers need to attach the byline to a face. You will want them to recognize you in your office, coffee shop or at the store.

Your newsletter is the integration of your writing style, your expertise, your business philosophy, your name and your face – all in one place. Readers will get to know *you* through your newsletter.

Make Them Laugh

"Laughter is the best medicine." It can also be the best marketing technique as well!

I can never remember a joke, but I always remember the person who made me laugh. Of course the main benefit of humor isn't just the laughs. Humor keeps people's attention, endears relationships and increases learning.

Humor in your newsletters will have the same effect. It breaks up the format of facts. No matter how informative your newsletters are, by inserting humor, it helps your readers remember what they've just read.

Don't be afraid to be a little silly. Your personal stories are the secret sauce in being funny. Don't try to be a comedian unless you're good at it – just tell some funny things that have happened to you.

There's a small section in every edition of *Reader's Digest* called "Life's Like That." It's the perfect example of how to engage humor in your newsletter. These are small stories with a humorous ending taken from everyday life experiences. The kinds of things that happen to us on a regular basis.

It's the story of working like crazy to not spill anything while you are painting your house. Finally, as you complete the task, you proudly announce to your spouse that you've painted the entire room without getting so much as a drop on anything. Then, as you step off the ladder, you place your foot squarely in the paint tray…

Include these kinds of stories to keep readers coming back. Remember what I stated in an earlier chapter: Flaws make you real. Don't neglect to tell your funny stories.

Frequency Matters

The frequency with which you send out your newsletters really matters. I recommend delivering your printed newsletters on at least a monthly basis.

Monthly newsletters offer just the right balance between frequency and depth of content. Your readers will have had enough time since the previous issue to digest the information and act on offers you included. They will also have had enough time to miss your entertaining insight. They will now be primed to receive the next newsletter in the mail.

A quarterly newsletter can be a great way for you to go in-depth on a host of issues. Unfortunately, you run the risk of your clients forgetting who you are between newsletters. If at all possible, aim for something more frequent, but quarterly is better than not at all.

In the electronic world, many organizations deliver emails weekly or even multiple times a week. The dilemma with "too many - too often" is over-saturation. Since they are delivered electronically, they run the risk of being deleted or banished to a holding folder, never to be read again.

Hard Copy Preferred

The argument for emailing a newsletter has always been its cost. Yes, emailed newsletters can be significantly less costly than printing and mailing a hard copy version. Also, there are those who respond positively to the fact that you didn't fill their mailbox with more paper. "Free" does not always mean "effective" though.

Email newsletters can be easily filtered by automatic spam software, deleted or hit with "read later" inbox rules. You don't want your hard work accidentally making its way to the virtual trash bin. You want your readers to pick up the newsletter, open it, read the headlines, see your picture and experience the whole thing before they decide if they are going to read it now or later.

It is very rare that someone sits down at a computer and reads an entire e-newsletter page by page and word for word. In fact, most people skim content when they read it online, even if it's something they'd normally be interested in reading.

With a hard copy, subscribers can flip through it as they would a magazine or newspaper, and read the stories that grab their eye. They'll return to the other stuff later because they have that hard copy on hand. An electronic copy will get a once over, and then never get looked at again.

Readers will likely want to *keep* your physical newsletter. They may even hang on to it so they can reference it at a later time. Readers are much more likely to pass it along to colleagues, friends and family. Studies have shown that a physical newsletter has three times the pass along value. They may just like it so much that they can't bear to throw it away.

No Hard Sell

Do not, I repeat, do not attempt to hard sell in your newsletter. If you forcefully, directly, or overtly try to sell to your readers, they are going to turn tail and never pick up your newsletter again.

Newsletters are a way for readers to get to know you and to become familiar with who you are and what you know. In fact, newsletters are the ultimate soft sell, because of their higher perceived value.

When you repeatedly and consistently convey your message to your subscribers without a selling stance, they will gradually be persuaded, rather than forced to make a decision.

You are helping customers and clients connect the dots through your newsletters so that all signs will point towards you as the person to do business with.

Be Prepared

Newsletters are work. They take time and money to create. Using them as a communication strategy needs 100% buy-in from you in order to be successful.

Newsletters are a commitment. Commit to sending them out once a month. Commit to providing information subscribers literally cannot find anywhere else. Commit to putting your personality in every word, in every picture, in every fold.

Newsletters are a form of creativity. Many of us rarely get to experience this type of creativity. With newspapers and magazines, you have to adhere to certain journalistic conventions. Although, with newsletters, you can be as outrageous, as humorous, as "out of the box" as you like. You are the writer, editor, and publisher – so have fun with it. The joy in your newsletter will be contagious to your readers. They'll have as much fun reading it as you had creating it.

> *The secret of becoming a writer is to write, write and keep on writing.*
> Ken MacLeod

CHAPTER 11

A Logo Advertises

I am one who believes that one of the greatest dangers of advertising is not that of misleading people, but that of boring them to death.
Leo Burnett

I know what you're thinking: "Traditional advertising?! I thought that's exactly what we weren't going to do."

The problem with this type of advertising (what I've been referring to as brand-based advertising) is that it focuses on the wrong thing – namely, the company and the brand.

In this chapter, you will discover how this type of advertising can work for *you* as the personality. Advertising, in a You Are The Logo way, relies on engaging yourself as the spokesperson for your business more than any other style.

The advertising tactics that I am describing here may not be suitable for your particular situation. You must be strategic in your use of larger scale ad media as there is a tendency to believe that the reach that they offer will solve all your marketing problems. Be aware to tread cautiously as the investment is often much larger in advertising than in other areas – however, in the right situations, it can be highly effective.

TV Commercials

I used to wonder why automobile dealers would star on their own TV spots. In my opinion, they were a little bit dense and quite cheesy. It wasn't until I began studying this type of advertising that I learned there was method to their madness. Not only were they creating a name for themselves, but they were positioning themselves to appear as if they were average people – people who could be out-negotiated. The problem is that they rarely are. Most car dealers that I've met are extremely sophisticated business people. Their ads work and continue to get people into their dealerships.

There are lots of opportunities to be a spokesperson for your local business without having to use the format some car dealers use. Watch your local TV stations to get a feel for the different styles of spokesperson ads in order to determine a style that authentically suits you.

Business leaders like Dan Hesse of Sprint, Dave Thomas of Wendy's and Christine Magee of Sleep Country Canada all starred in successful TV commercials for their businesses.

Frank Perdue revolutionized advertising when he appeared as one of the first CEOs to take on the role of public spokesperson. His "It takes a tough man to make a tender chicken" ads turned Perdue Farms into the first well-known brand of chicken in the United States.

Spokesperson marketing on TV works. The Nielsen Company – which monitors viewing habits – reports that 99% of all American households watch TV on a regular basis. The average American spends four to five hours *a day* watching television. By the time a person is 65 years old, they'll have viewed over two million 30-second commercials.

For the right company, this can be a huge opportunity to advertise your business using the power of your personality.

Radio Commercials

Charles Osgood, the CBS broadcaster wrote, "What makes radio such a terrific 'telling' medium also makes it a terrific 'selling' medium."

For a personality marketer, this is good news. There are commercials playing on the radio for every type of business, from lawyers to salons – to heating and cooling services – and from auto dealers to furniture stores. At its heart, radio advertising is simple and effective. It's just your voice going out over the local airwaves. Ads allow you to be the spokesperson for your business.

Make these ads personal and connect yourself to a call to action.

Another avenue into radio advertising is to be a guest on a talk show or even host your own half-hour to hour-long weekend talk show. In most cases, you pay for the time slot and create your show. Hosting your own show or being a regular guest on another show quickly positions you as the expert in your field.

Dr. Dawn Motyka hosts an hour-long health show on California station KUSP every Saturday. Len Tillem is a lawyer and host of a very popular legal program on San Francisco station KKSF. There are numerous examples of personalities on the radio in cities everywhere who do it as the front-end of their business.

Radio is much more cost effective than TV, but is only worthwhile if it establishes you and your business to your target prospect market. As with all advertising mediums, radio has to allow you to reach your target market and get a result to be effective.

Newspaper Advertising

Flip through any newspaper and you'll notice that few ads feature an actual human being, let alone a business personality. Every so often though, there are extremely successful ads that feature a personality pitching their business in print. The ad can be as straightforward as a picture of the personality with a caption that reads, "You've got my personal guarantee."

Newspaper readership, especially the print versions, is dwindling. This makes your choice to invest in print ads a difficult decision. If your target market is prone to read them, then it would be worthwhile.

"Advertorials" have long proven to be a great methodology for business personalities to market themselves in print newspapers. These are pages of advertising that have the look of an editorial piece and can feature a business personality prominently as its centerpiece.

Magazine Advertising

Printed in color on glossy, beautifully designed pages, magazines offer a pop that many newspapers lack. Yet, as more magazines have gone national, the ability to advertise in a cost-effective way has diminished. However, if you dig a little, you'll be surprised at how many publications there are in almost every niche or category. They may not have the scope or readership of the ones found at the grocery store checkout, but they might be the right readers for you.

Billboards

If you need your local prospects to see you "larger than life," then billboards can work for you. The key with billboards is abundance. They work when prospective clients see your face everywhere they turn. Billboards offer additional exposure because you are literally out in the elements. Your name, face, phone number and website are all out there for the public to see.

A prominent Jacksonville, Florida-based attorney, Eddie Farah, has billboards scattered all over Jacksonville. They're well thought out, legible, have a high production value and solidify his identity within his marketplace. Eddie doesn't rely solely on billboards but uses them as part of his overall personality marketing strategy.

If you use billboards – or other location based media like bus stop ads or sitting bench back ads – you must be sure it compliments your more significant advertising in other media as well.

Direct Mail

The mailbox remains one of the most effective ways to get in front of your targeted audience at a very reasonable cost. In addition, it is a great media to engage your Logo personality. As others get scared away from using mail due to the increasing postage costs, you can get in front of your prospective clients in very interesting ways.

The insight to remember is that everybody looks at his or her mail. Opening the mail is something most people do after arriving home at night or in the office. Granted, getting past the administrative assistant in the office is a little more challenging than if sent to a home, but it is still one of my favorite ways to get in front of my prospect market.

Here are the best practices:

- You need to have a great mailing list. Without the right list, you are completely wasting your money.
- You need to create compelling copy that is relevant to the people on the list. Generic copy will not do. It must be tailored for the person opening it.
- You need to have an attractive offer or an opportunity that they can act on. You must inspire them to act.
- You need to ensure that the recipient receives your mailer, opens it and reads it.
- You need to be persistent, sequential and repetitious. Don't send a single mail piece and expect a response or return. I recommend (at minimum) three consecutive pieces to even get noticed.

Other than that, it's easy!!!

If you've gotten the best practices right, the fun part of direct mail is the capacity to add your personality. You get to be your quirky, lighthearted, nerdy, expert, or charming self. Your recipients love to be entertained!

Use the opportunities that mail provides to engage many of the ideas that we shared in the first half of the book. Grab the reader emotionally and move them along the path so they eagerly want to do business with you. Add your picture, tell your stories, and be interesting. Most of all, don't underestimate this media.

Web Advertising

The web is a huge advertising opportunity all by itself. Entire books have been written on how to use single elements of the Internet marketing world like Google AdWords, Facebook marketing and Search Engine Optimization.

Please recognize, however, that web-based advertising demands as much strategy and rigor in assessing its effectiveness as you might give TV, radio and print-based advertising. While the lure of it might be its free nature, web marketing is complex and demands significant investment, either through third party support or your own time. The benefits are its reach and its ability to track activity and results most efficiently and immediately.

On top of that, web marketing is an amazing place to be the Logo for your business. There are so many extraordinary opportunities online to market yourself and your business using many of the tactics we've already discussed in this book: web video for speaking, educating and training; blogs and third party sites for writing; social media for networking and relationship building. The list goes on and on. Use it to its fullest potential.

Always remember that the Internet is just another medium. You can advertise effectively – or you can spend money foolishly. It is no better or worse than other advertising tools. It just depends on how it is used and what you are trying to accomplish. Don't get seduced into using the Internet as the only way to market and advertise your business while neglecting some of the other opportunities outlined in this chapter and throughout this book.

Reinforce Your Position

I can't emphasize enough the importance of ubiquity. Effective advertising is all about reinforcing your position and your reputation. It allows you to attract new clients in as many media places as fits your strategy and that you are able to support economically.

When you pair advertising with other personality-building strategies such as speaking engagements, writing, publicity and more, your prospective clients and customers won't have to hunt you down. You will be right in front of them and ready to do business.

> *Forget words like 'hard sell' and 'soft sell.' That will only confuse you. Just be sure your advertising is saying something with substance, something that will inform and serve the consumer, and be sure you're saying it like it's never been said before.*
> William Bernbach

CHAPTER 12

A Logo Publicizes

*The only thing worse than being talked about
is NOT being talked about.*
Oscar Wilde

Do you know the old saying, "No press is bad press?"
Getting your name mentioned by the news media in newspapers, blogs or magazines, or getting them to interview you by recording or videotaping, will boost your visibility and overall presence as the personality for your business.

Being good at generating publicity allows you to gain a notoriety not found in some of the other tactics already mentioned. Done well, publicity means the media will take notice of you and the issues you champion. People will recognize you, remember you, and know you, ultimately wanting to do business with you.

A wonderful part about media coverage is its ability to corroborate your credibility. Readers often see press coverage as neutral, third party and objective – so they place enormous trust in it. When you are profiled or written about, you gain the benefit of name recognition, heightened prestige, and the perception that you are a leader in your field.

Finally, one of the benefits offered by media coverage is the ability to leverage the coverage you get for yourself and your business. Media is quick to come and quick to go. So it is critical that the media coverage you do receive gets captured for reuse in all your other marketing. Collect it, archive it and reuse it repeatedly as more proof of your expertise, your standing or your celebrity.

What the Media Want

The media and the public love characters. They don't want bland, boring personalities. When was the last time you saw someone like that in the headlines on a news talk show? If you had seen those types of personalities, what was your reaction to them?

Donald Trump receives exceptional press coverage because he creates something to talk about. Not only is he newsworthy, he will often say bold or brash things that cause controversy. He is not wishy-washy. You shouldn't be either.

Have a Powerful Position

Take a stand. Have an opinion. The press and the public won't bother paying attention to you if you're a middle-of-the-roader. Have an interesting argument with a compelling reason that you can passionately present to the reading and viewing public.

Joan Rivers has never been one to stay quiet about her opinions. Even as she nears 80 she still lands spots on talk shows and appears on sold-out comedy tours. She's a lightening rod of publicity. You don't have to be the center of controversy or a polarizing figure, but you do need to take a strong stand on the issues you encounter in your business and industry.

Media companies know that controversy fuels readership, watchers or listeners, so they want those who will not only have an opinion but also express it.

In the two TV series that I produced and hosted, I looked for guests who had a strong opinion. As a guest host on a daytime talk show, it was the strong characters who received the most response from the audience. As a producer, the goal of programming is to have viewers or listeners that create feedback – the more the better.

How To Get Publicity

Media or Press Releases

You're throwing a fundraiser for a local charity. You're appearing before a government committee to testify on an important industry issue. You're doing something out of the ordinary with your business. How do you get media coverage of the event?

Media and press releases are a traditional but still effective way to get the media's attention. Despite claims to the contrary, many local editors and reporters continue to rely on press releases to learn about the things that they eventually write stories about or cover as news items.

Most newspapers and other media outlets welcome press releases because they need to fill their pages with content – just as much as you need to fill your charity event with donors.

Remember that your press release is not a sales pitch. You don't write a press release to sell your product or service. You write a press release to give the reporter or media outlet a story to relay to their audience. You provide them ideas and content so they can more easily use you or your perspective to support what they will be delivering in their piece.

Realize that you are not the only one submitting these press releases.

Editors and reporters are inundated with them daily. If you want to be noticed, you need to stand out from the stack with an intriguing or interesting headline and a story that catches their attention.

Spend a little time on the PR Newswire site and you will see just how many press releases are being created every minute of the day. The ones posted on this site are by those who are willing to pay to get their press release posted – and were in most cases – written by professionals. Then dig into every fourth or fifth one. If you take the time to read them, it doesn't take long to realize how boring most of these professionally written press releases can be.

Imagine what a local news editor receives? How can you possibly stand out?

Then spend a few more minutes on a free press release website such as *free-press-release.com* and look into just one category, say "Business." Dig into just three or four press releases part way down the page. What I believe you will witness is the sheer volume being generated and the complete lack of story they provide.

You cannot get stuck in this mess!

The World Is Changing

While traditional press releases are the old standby, the media (or what's left of them) are now incredibly web savvy. If you only rely on traditional press releases – even if you are delivering them via web-based press release sites – you are missing even bigger opportunities.

The social media world has created an environment where everyone is a journalist and everyone can be a media outlet. In this context, you must also see publicity as a targeted approach to the online media personalities who have established clout – either in terms of followers or some other type of influence – in your specific niche or locale.

You cannot use the traditional press release format to get in front of established online media personalities. You need to be more creative in getting them to take notice of you. Start with building a simple relationship in a social media environment. "Follow" or "Friend" them on Twitter, Facebook, Google+ or LinkedIn and attempt to start a simple dialog before you "pitch" them.

Your goal is still the same. You want them to deliver to their established audience something about you such that their readers or followers take notice and give you their attention. However, if you start with that as your request, the door to their audience will most likely be closed. Provide them with value that matters to them, give them resources or support them in some way in advance. You are more likely to get your desired result this way.

You Become The Media Outlet

The direction we're headed means something different. Essentially, you are the publisher of the future. An entire chapter is dedicated to this concept later in the book, but as it relates to publicity, companies can actually become the sole creator of the articles, news and content they want delivered and not rely on the traditional press to cover it.

Over the last few years larger brands are bringing reporters in house or hiring journalists – instead of PR experts – to create their own media machines. If you haven't seen or heard about American Express OPEN Forum, this is an established company that has now become a publisher. Their readers and viewers are going directly to them to consume the information, bypassing the traditional sources.

The key is to be a content generator. In the old model (press release-focused) we pitched the media to notice us and then hoped they would create the content that generated buzz or credibility on our behalf. Even in the social model, the goal was to get others to talk about us. This is still all valuable.

But the emerging model is one where the content you produce and deliver is actually consumed by your "niche" audience without ever needing to visit the former middle-man – the press. As you take on the role of publisher and deliver your own message, your world begins to talk about you and the things you are doing and providing. They gain value and pass it on.

No longer is your focus how to write a press release and hope that a journalist tells it or relays it in a way that supports you. The new emerging model is that you tell your story about you and your business that prospects want to read. You become the media.

Chris Brogan is a New York Times Bestselling Author and Founder of PodCamp, a new media conference series. He is also the President of Human Business Works. Chris is a prolific content producer on his websites and uses social media channels to link back to his content. *Advertising Age* ranks Chris as one of the top bloggers in the world. He is a great example of becoming the media outlet.

Publicity Options

Be The Feature Story

Feature stories are often the centerpiece of a publication and almost always get profiled on the front page or cover. Websites also have feature stories. You'll notice media websites frequently display one, two or three feature stories prominently on their main pages.

These types of stories are longer than normal articles. They go in-depth and tell the full story of the topic. A reporter will often spend hours or more with their subject as they get to the core of who they are and what they do. They can be a real gold mine for you.

Features offer amazing exposure as well as increase your visibility. This means you are interesting enough to have 1,500+ words dedicated to you – not to mention some dynamic photos – a bio and a link to your website included in the article.

A number of years ago, my local newspaper, *The KW Record*, did a feature story on me. My story and picture filled three quarters of the cover page of the "Life" section of the paper. The full-length story written by the reporter – and the placement of it on the cover of the section – gave me immediate credibility. The story was about my profession at the time, a professional speaker. The day it was published, I received at least five calls by organizations looking for speakers. Within days I had received even more.

Be A Contributor to a Story

"No press is bad press," so getting your name in the text of an article is a great way to gain publicity and the attention that comes with it. It can be a valuable tool to build your publicity proof package. As a contributor, you still get recognition and in most cases, as a contributor, your role is to be the expert. This supports your positioning and your credibility.

If you get to know a reporter that covers your industry, rather than feeding them press releases, get to know them and become a trusted resource and subject matter expert.

Wayne Hussey is a strategic planning expert, as well as a consultant in the areas of human resources and fundraising. I asked Wayne to be a contributor to my TV show, *Adams & Company*, on a weekly basis. He and I would chat briefly about important business improvement principles via remote video as we recorded the show each week. Wayne became invaluable to the show as his unique contribution allowed me to deliver better content to my viewers – and at the same time, it increased his own positioning as an expert in the business community.

Guest on Radio or TV

We see and hear CEOs and other business personalities do this all the time.

> "Today on CNBC's Squackbox, we'll be talking to Ron Peltier, CEO of HomeServices of America about today's housing crisis."

> "Next on the Drive at Five, as you're stuck in traffic cursing the other drivers, we're going to talk to the Stress Doctor."
>
> "Hi folks, welcome to Wake Up Wisconsin. On the program today we'll be talking to local business owner Shirley Swanson of Swings and More. She's started a campaign to get rid of the evil lurking in your local park playgrounds."

Contact local television and radio stations about your willingness and availability to be a guest. As you build your presence, making compelling, newsworthy announcements and championing causes that grab producers' attention, you'll get invited to appear on their programs.

These appearances are normally no longer then 5-10 minutes. Be prepared with some distinct talking points or short "sound bites." Have fun, be lively, and remember that hundreds or more prospective clients are being introduced to you for the first time through these interviews. Interviewers love to have your potential questions provided in advance of the interview to help them know what to ask.

Get the Spotlight

To get publicity and press, you have to be extraordinary. There's got to be something about you – a spark, a light, an energy – that draws reporters and other media members to you.

Amplify your personality. Showcase your strengths and be honest about your flaws. The press will respect you for it.

> *High-level, big-deal publicity has a way of getting old for me, but what never fails to thrill me is when I make personal appearances.*
> **Joseph Barbera**

Don't turn away from the spotlight. Not every single detail of your life has to be included in the press, but each time your name is in print or your picture pops up online or you're on the radio, business prospects will take notice. They'll want to be doing business with the person they're hearing so much about.

CHAPTER 13

A Logo Associates

*Surround yourself with only people
who are going to lift you higher.*
Oprah Winfrey

There's an old adage, "It's not so much *what* you know but *who* you know that counts."
In the context of criminal activity, people are often judged to be "guilty by association." In this world of personality-based marketing, you are judged by the relationships you have and the company you keep.
In building a powerful position and a definitive reputation, the people you hang out with – and the circles you associate with –have an incredible impact on your standing and the perceptions your prospective clients make about you.

This part of your Logo efforts is not to be left to chance. It requires that you be diligent about crafting an authentic reputation for yourself based on the people and organizations with whom you associate.

Your Clients and Customers

This may seem like a very basic principle, but your clients and customers define you. If effective marketing happens when you choose a niche, then the type of clients you begin to work with inside of that niche will clarify your positioning even more.

So, if you work with clients who trust your unique perspective, who value your service offering and who are willing to pay extra for you to deliver the best in class results, your status will be elevated. The better your clients, the more likely you are to get more of them. We discussed attraction earlier in the book and identified that similarity, proximity and familiarity all are factors in attraction. You tend to attract more of the same kind of client or customer as you already have.

I have always been intrigued by the pictures on the walls of certain restaurants. You know the ones… where the owner of the restaurant is photographed with every celebrity who has ever eaten at the place?

I recall during my college days going to Ed's Warehouse, a once-famous Toronto landmark restaurant in the theater district (owned by Ed Mirvisch, a true Logo). I remember viewing a wall of hundreds of pictures that included Ed and a cast of celebrities that had eaten in his restaurant over the years. Somehow as I stood there in that moment, I felt like I was one of them. I too, was eating at Ed's.

The psychology of identifying your optimal clients and then finding a way to make them known can be a significant attraction mechanism to others who are similar.

Testimonials and client lists are great ways to establish a baseline portrait of who is collectively your client base. In the direct marketing world, you use testimonials to provide social proof that you are a competent and reliable provider which is very important. However, the pictures on your wall – and the testimonials that you share – are also adept ways of positioning yourself in the minds of your prospect community.

Your Personal Network

Any successful owner, executive or professional will attest to the power of a network. For many, your network helped you get to where you are today in business. Rather simplistically, you are your network. It defines you.

I want you to see it as something more than the traditional "show up at a Chamber meeting," shake some hands and introduce yourself. This is not about just having a name, number or email address in your virtual Rolodex. There are those out there who can claim a huge amount of Friends, Connections or Followers in their social networks. Yet, while those might be efficient doorways to build a network, they lack the depth required to actually *possess* a viable network.

As the Logo for your business, building a network is about creating highly effective relationships that form the foundation of someone's ability to know, like and trust you. Harvey Mackay's excellent book, *Dig Your Well Before You Are Thirsty*, encourages us to think differently about the whole concept of networking.

> "What if you were facing a business issue that required you to call someone at two in the morning to request his or her help? Have you built those kinds of relationships in your business network? Have you established the kind of relationships with others that allow them to call you if the same were true?"

In each opportunity to build your network, Mackay encourages his readers to dig their well a little deeper, and to ensure it is continually deepened, such that thirst is never an issue. In order to do so, you must provide positive value to every encounter with people, whether it is a new relationship or enhancing an existing one.

A really deep well comes not just from a small group of highly committed friends and colleagues. It is constructed from a wide variety of different and diverse relationships, not all of the same variety. Don't just network with your client community but also with other vendors who serve them as you do. Improve and deepen the relationships with your current vendors and build more established relationships with those you don't purchase goods or services from.

While the act of networking and building relationships within the context of this book is written as a tactical tool, the point is not about doing it so you have a sales target list. It's about being the kind of person who builds solid relationships and networks because of the value it provides to others. When done for purely selfish reasons, networking will never dig your well.

When you build relationships that establish trust and provide value to others, the rewards to you will become self-evident in due time. While it's naïve to think that people do not enter a relationship without expecting to get something out of it, the more we invest in the building and deepening of relationships, the more we tend to get from them. The best time to build and cement relationships is when you don't need it, and they do. You'll find that when you willingly step up and support people who need it, in time it will come back to you.

As you establish and build your business and social network in this context, you become known and your reputation is solidified.

Community or Industry Involvement

Networking is the way to build and establish relationships, while involvement in your community or industry further solidifies your positioning as a leader, expert or philanthropist. It is imperative that you associate with a community of some kind as a Logo.

Rotary Clubs, PTA meetings, charitable events, local business associations, whichever you choose – get out in your community and contribute. If your client base is national, get involved in the industry associations or groups to which your clients belong. This is as much a community as something local.

There are always opportunities to contribute value in these settings. Within this context, you will meet people who are also contributing. As you work alongside them, your relationships will grow as will your reputation.

Another level of contribution and network building can take place when you choose to be part of the leadership in your respective community. This demands more extensive time and energy, but the rewards can be even greater. You can contribute your unique perspective and expertise to a particular board of directors. You can be involved in less formal advisory boards. You can bring your talents and perspective to groups that need them and will benefit.

The value you deliver to the community as a leader, and the opportunity to help shape a community, an industry or a not-for-profit agency is reward in and of itself. Add to that the relationships formed around boardroom tables – whether they are in a business or not for profit environment – and you will build enhanced networks. The derivative value of being involved in a leadership position is the continual advancement and reputation you build for yourself.

Referral, Affiliate and Joint Venture Networks

There is important leverage that comes from associating with people who can – and will – send others to you and your business. This has long been a preferred methodology within small town business communities. If you went to the hardware store and asked the owner for a certain item that they didn't carry, they would know where to send you to get it. Referrals between those who wished to see each other succeed are built on the personal networking we have already discussed.

As a Logo, one of your immediate tasks is to learn where you can refer your clients and prospects for all manner of services. *What kinds of things do your clients and customers need that you cannot provide?* Then begin to build a list of referrals.

Mohandas Gandhi said "Be the change you wish to see in the world." In the case of getting referrals, it means being someone who actively sends referrals. The hope is that as you become someone who gives referrals, you will then receive them back.

Hope, however, is not a good strategy in a referral context. You must build a number of different ways to get others to send customers your way. Affiliate marketing is one such way. Essentially, an affiliate relationship boils down to referrals and compensation. An affiliate in your network is someone who directs prospects to your business and receives financial compensation for doing so.

Brokers, manufacturer's agents or representatives have long been in this business. They have a number of product lines they carry and with their established client networks, they seek to fulfill their client's needs through selling whatever product lines they carry. When they sell the product, they are paid a commission.

Affiliate marketing works by the same premise. The goal is to find those best positioned within your target prospect community to recommend you to their existing client lists. If you are in the electrical business, you would want to establish affiliate agreements with plumbers and HVAC business owners. The compensation for these referrals would be the incentive for these companies to continue to do it.

In the online world, affiliate marketing is completely automated. With simple software, people can become affiliates and send clients to you without ever establishing a relationship with you personally. The entire goal on their part is the commission gained from just getting their existing audience to take their advice and purchase a product or service from you. This automation is much more difficult offline, but the premise remains the same. People want to be rewarded for sending their client or followers to you.

Within this referral context, there is a deeper level of association that can be developed into joint ventures. Joint ventures are partnerships where two or more parties come together to accomplish a particular task.

Health or wellness centers can be a great example of this. A doctor might be the anchor partner surrounded by a massage therapist, a chiropractor, a nutritionist and a psychologist or a counselor. Collaboratively, each of the practitioners works to grow their own practice while they also work towards a common goal of growing the center's overall client base. They actively refer within the joint venture partnership so that they all benefit.

Endorsements

One of the highest and most important associations you can make for yourself is to have well-known people, experts with well-established reputations, organizations or those with celebrity status vouch for you by endorsing you.

This is often more powerful than a testimonial or even a simple referral. Endorsements can be merely implied or more explicitly given, but, either way, it is extremely advantageous for you to receive it.

As discussed earlier in the book, we live in a celebrity-focused culture. It is very apparent that much of the population endows celebrities with wisdom that is not always justified, but is evident nonetheless. People generally believe that if a celebrity endorses something then it must be good.

Companies and brands work tirelessly to get celebrities to wear or use their products. Watch the red carpet interviews before an awards show and you'll see how important clothing and jewelry endorsements are. Watch the green room footage afterward and you will catch glimpses of the abundant gifts the celebrities receive. This is done with the hopes that something included in the gift baskets will catch their eye and, as a result of using or wearing it, their implied endorsement will occur.

In the example of the restaurant, the owner's picture with their celebrity guest is implied endorsement. The celebrity chose to eat in that particular restaurant, therefore the restaurant must be good. This is not always a true statement but it is one that is often believed. This is why taking pictures of celebrities in your restaurant is a valuable thing to do.

In addition, paid endorsements by celebrities are a strong option to consider. You might not have the budget to get A-list, or even B-list, celebrities, but there may be local celebrities you can negotiate deals with to endorse you. Radio talk show hosts are great for this.

In my former home city of Kitchener, just outside of Toronto, my favorite morning radio announcer was Dave Sturgeon. He was very adept at giving endorsements as a local media celebrity; Dave learned golf; lost weight; drove specific kinds of cars; and wore clothes from certain stores. All of this was part of his paid role in endorsing these businesses.

Yet, endorsements do not always need to come from celebrities. They can come from experts or even from an organization. If you are asked to speak to a group, that is implied endorsement from that group.

Remember that who you associate with is a compelling way to elevate and establish you as the Logo for your business. Your clients, your network, your community involvement, your referral partners and endorsers all serve to elevate you to a positioning that creates even more effective marketing.

CHAPTER 14

A Logo Publishes

The names are bigger, the show is worldwide, but I get a royal pass into life in the broadcasting business.
Larry King

You can gain an admiral "personal" reputation by leveraging this proven approach, which is that *you* become the publisher or broadcaster. You use existing media delivery options such as radio, TV, print and the Internet to establish a publishing platform for yourself. This platform becomes the way to establish a position in the marketplace that leverages many of the Logo tactics we've discussed in the book already.

Tom Does TV

Almost 20 years ago, I was trying to establish a business reputation in my local market in Ottawa, Canada. I knew that based on my limited experience and capabilities, I would not be able to speak to decision makers about my ability to support them with the services I provided. I realized I needed to do things in a very different way.

I approached my local television station, and pitched them on an idea to create a local business-focused TV show that profiled the most interesting and successful companies in the area. My goal was to interview business leaders whose companies were making a difference in the community.

The local station saw value in my idea and gave me a 30-minute, 16-week show and provided me with a support crew and technical producer to make it happen.

Having had absolutely no experience in TV production, I needed to wing-it. I created a list of owners and executives in the community, and then decided on a list of people I wanted to get to know. I assumed that getting them to meet with me would be as difficult and as frustrating as cold calling had been. To my astonishment, I was wrong.

It was amazing to me that, from a sales perspective, doors that were seemingly closed before I had a TV show, immediately opened up when I approached them as a media person. When I called the companies and asked to speak to the president or owner, I was granted immediate access.

My first TV show, *Making A Difference*, was born out of my attempt to create some name recognition for myself, and it worked! I met some incredibly cool people.

A few years later I moved to a new city and realized that if my consulting business was to gain clients, I needed to get visible once again. Recalling the results of my first series, I tried it again. I approached the local TV station and pitched them on my show idea, *Adams & Company*, where I would profile "world-class fast and funky companies and the people that made them that way." I got approval to do the show. With the knowledge gained from my first show – and a clearer objective for the outcome – I went to work on my second TV series.

This show not only created incredible connections, but it also created a significant amount of residual business for me. More importantly, it created life-long business allies and relationships that continue to have ongoing value to my business. The show was broadcast on the entire Canadian network and as a result, provided me with substantial name recognition and even more press.

All of this was before we had the power of the Internet to leverage what I was doing in an even bigger way. In the age of the Internet, the opportunity to exponentially increase the value of this publishing tactic has been used by many to solidify their own business presence.

The Scoble Effect

Robert Scoble is a former Microsoft employee who has become one of the most influential online media personalities in the world. He is a well-known blogger and technology reporter that has hundreds of thousands of followers. He's actually been credited with creating a surge in business for many start-up Internet companies just by interviewing them or posting an endorsement of them – affectionately called the "Scoble Effect." He's had stints with companies such as PodTech and Fast Company over the years.

In 2009, Robert was hired by Rackspace to be their public face. He is paid to create media on behalf of the company, which by the way is not focused on promoting Rackspace. Instead, they pay him to discover, profile and interview all sorts of companies in the technology space.

What's so intriguing about this whole story with Rackspace and Robert is what it's actually done for the company. When he was hired in 2009, the stock of Rackspace was trading at $5.98/share. Today, the share price hovers around $40.

You might assume that the increase in their share price came from a variety of other reasons unrelated to Scoble's publishing presence within the business. Although that could be true, the best way to measure his significance and impact on Rackspace is to do an experiment of sorts. Mark Fidelman actually conducted such an experiment and here were his findings:

> "While we can't with certainty state that there's an association between Scoble's arrival and RAX's superior stock performance, we can note that prior to Scoble's arrival RAX maintained price parity with its competitors. Shortly after his arrival however, RAX broke from the pack and has maintained a superior return."

Scoble's impact remains constant. There is such amazing opportunity to build a personal reputation in a niche or industry or local community using the power of becoming the publisher within the industry. Rackspace is a media company – not just a hosting company. Robert Scoble is their Logo.

Pepsi as Publisher

At last year's South-by-Southwest Conference (SXSW is one of the most notable technology, music and film conferences in the world), Pepsi took the unusual role of publisher. Instead of merely being an advertiser, they became a publishing company.

They hired David Weiner – a noted PR expert – who along with a support team of interviewers – created a channel to serve up interviews with speakers, tech celebrities and attendees. The result was that PepsiCo became the media channel for the entire conference, and in doing so, they outperformed and outwitted the traditional reporters. Local attendees were watching the online channel but even more importantly – so was the world.

You Are The Logo Media Company

The wonderful advantage you possess today is that the creation of your own media company is less about economics and more about just making the decision to do it. Before YouTube and embedded webcams and microphones, creating a video or audio channel would have cost a fortune. You needed cameras and equipment. You needed software and high-end editing expertise. Today, you can record video directly to YouTube and edit it online.

So the opportunity is as available to *you* as it is to everyone. The question is, will you take advantage of it? Will you publish as the media creator and channel owner?

I refer you back to Gary Vaynerchuk. Gary became the noted wine industry publisher and media channel. His show WineLibraryTV.com helped his reputation to explode and clearly impacted the economics of his wine business.

Two years ago, I created a podcast for a niche industry that my company still serves. On the weekly show I interview various people, including members of the industry as well as vendors to the industry. My goal is simply to share their stories. It is not investigative journalism.

The podcast takes significant amounts of planning, set-up and interview time, as well as editing plus the requirement to promote the show. However, the value to me and my business is tremendous.

Just as the Rackspace numbers indicated, owning the media channel has a direct impact on my own business results. My podcast creates positioning, reputation and attraction that supports ongoing sales within my business.

I encourage you to look for a way to create your own media channel and then publish as much as you can. This can be an amazing way to enhance your reputation and put you in an advantageous position in your market or community.

CHAPTER 15

A Logo Engages

*The big question is whether you are going to be able to say
a hearty yes to your big adventure.*
Joseph Campbell

You Are The Logo is all about putting your face and personality into the forefront of your business marketing.

The first half of this book provided proof and reasons as well as ways of thinking and preparing you to become the Logo for your business. The second half of the book focused on the tools and tactics you can use to elevate and distinguish yourself in order to gain a ubiquitous presence in your marketplace. These include opportunities in speaking, writing, advertising, publicizing, associating and publishing.

Your next move is to engage in the process and to move toward implementation.

Take Chances, Get Messy, Make Mistakes

When my sons were toddlers, there was a cartoon show on TV they watched that taught science in an innovative way. The show was called the *Magic School Bus* and took place in the context of the science classroom. "Ms. Frizzle" was the teacher in the school as well as the driver of the magic bus which took her classroom students on magnificent field trips to impossible locations such as the solar system, into the clouds, the past, and even inside the human body.

Ms. Frizzle would often encourage the kids in her class to explore their world and not be afraid. The line she repeated that sticks in my head to this day is, "Take Chances. Get Messy. Make Mistakes!"

As you embark on this wonderful marketing adventure where You Are The Logo, there is no official roadmap. I've shared the context and philosophy for what to do, but the actual doing of it requires you to jump in and see what happens. Take some chances. Expect that you might get messy along the way. Know that you will likely make some mistakes as you do – but the rewards can be great if you learn and grow along the way.

Start with small things and grow from there. Write a simple blog post before you try to get published in the local business journal. Create a tip sheet for prospects before you try to write an entire tip book. Do a simple 30-second YouTube video with your webcam where you introduce yourself and your business before you try to do the big one on TV.

So while I want you to take the chances and get messy, I don't want you to ruin your clothes completely. Take chances where the impact is not going to hurt you or the business. Do experiments that will give you an indication of whether or not it will work for you.

Naysayers and Self-Doubt

Putting yourself into a public and visible position will inevitably mean someone dislikes you or what you do. Your competitors might complain or speak ill of you. Your spouse may think you have lost your mind. Your investors or business associates might suggest you are diminishing the brand reputation. All of this might be easy compared to what happens inside your own head.

There is an internal fight that happens within us when we choose to put ourselves out there very publicly. The questions arise: *Am I capable? Am I being too self-serving by focusing attention on myself?*

You might also hit on things related to your own appearance, your skills in public and the inevitable question, *"Will they like me?"*

Be aware that these are some roadblocks you might face along the way to being the Logo for your business. Despite ample proof that this approach works and is a proven marketing methodology – when no one else in your market is doing it – it may seem hard to go against the grain. It requires that you face your own internal self doubt and plot a path unique to you. I've been there and have experienced the roadblocks and assure you that they don't need to stop you.

Be Strategic

If you are in any way overwhelmed by all the options presented in this book, let me set your mind at ease. You can't do them all. Nor should you try. I recommend that you choose tactics that are aligned with a comprehensive marketing strategy.

You might want to be the recognized face of your company and appear on the commercials aired during the local TV news. However, if the only people watching the commercial are you and your friends, it won't do you much good.

The goal of any marketing campaign, whether it's a more traditional brand-based style – or our preferred You Are The Logo style – is to begin with a strategic plan that sets the course. Out of that strategy, you determine your implementation objectives and then formulate the required messages to match the prospects you are targeting. Your audience will help you to define which media you should choose to accompany the specific messages. You must also determine what resources you require to effectively implement your various campaigns.

In your planning, you will need to choose which tactics to use and which ones to avoid. Even if you have an unlimited budget, you might not have the time to engage all the possible options. As is often the case, there may be certain marketing tactics that are not appropriate for your situation. Your Logo style becomes important in the ones you engage.

The Power of Seven

It is clear that you can't and shouldn't try to use all marketing tactics at your disposal, but you should use enough to be effective. As we discussed in Chapter 4 on Marketing Refreshers, you gain stability through the diversity of your marketing tactics and activities.

While your entire business might be engaging 10-20 various marketing approaches, I encourage you to engage seven specific things to support the effective implementation of your own Logo activity. The magic in seven is that it requires you to push just slightly beyond your comfort zone.

My own activities relate to marketing the services my company offers to a unique niche, the records and information management support industry.

My seven Logo marketing tactics are:

1. **Speak.** At a number of industry conferences throughout the year I am invited to speak about marketing related topics.

2. **Publish.** I produce and host an industry podcast that airs weekly.

3. **Industry Involvement.** I am an active participant on

different committees within the industry association.

4. **Direct Mail.** I routinely send personalized, interesting and sequential campaigns to targeted members of my industry.

5. **Referrals.** I make it easy for my clients to refer me to others. Through well-established industry vendor partner relationships, I give and receive active referrals.

6. **Newsletter.** I publish and send a physical newsletter to my clients and prospects. It's a simple, four- page newsletter that gets distributed by postal mail each month.

7. **Educational Resources.** I have written articles and had them published in various industry magazines. I develop and publish free education resources including special reports and online videos.

I share these to give you a realistic idea of what you might possibly do. But please note, my seven tactics are shown as an example, not as a recommendation for what you should specifically do.

Get A Mirror That Doesn't Lie

Part of stepping into a more public role is that you will be held to a higher standard. You may be judged more harshly on certain things that you might not have to worry about with more brand-centered marketing.

Impressions matter. Perception often dictates how you are received. How you put yourself together might be the last thing you think of, but the first thing your prospects see and make instantaneous judgments about. When you work to achieve a powerful positioning and a definitive reputation, be sure to lead with a positive impression. There is a reason the celebrities have stylists. Despite how shallow it might seem, your personal style matters.

Be sure to find someone you trust and will be honest with you. It's easy to look in the mirror and miss the things that others see. If you are really unsure, hire someone who can help you with this.

Get an opinion about the clothes you wear.

- Are they appropriate in your context?
- Do they fit you well?
- Are they dated?
- How about personal grooming?
- What about your social skills and manners?
- Do your table skills undermine your expert status?

These are the questions that we don't like to consider but should be asked nevertheless. An image consultant can be a terrific resource to help you in this area.

Oh, The Places You'll Go

You are about to engage on a wonderful adventure. You will astound yourself with what you can do when you set your mind to it. There are so many things that you will discover as you become the Logo for your business.

My hope and dream for you is that this book fills you with a renewed energy to market your business. But more than that, I hope it challenges you to be a bigger YOU – to ask more of yourself than you have before – and then give yourself permission to do it. I hope that when you step up and allow yourself to shine, you'll surprise yourself with what you'll accomplish.

> *Once you've done all the mental work, there comes a point in time you have to throw yourself into the action and put your heart on the line.*
> Phil Jackson

Some day I hope we meet and you have the chance to tell me how much fun it's all been. I look forward to learning about your business success and the expanded platform you now possess to do even greater things. I can't wait to hear you enthusiastically say "I Am The Logo!"

Conclusion

You might be a little confused about what to do and where to start this journey to being the Logo for your business. You might even be a little concerned that you don't have what it takes to do so.

You're shy. You're not comfortable in public. You have a large head or funny ears or numerous other excuses that keep you from taking the next step.

In the 2011 movie, *We Bought a Zoo*, Benjamin Mee (played by Matt Damon) is sitting with his son Dylan on the floor near the tiger cage. Dylan is describing the awkwardness he has with Lily, a girl at the zoo. Benjamin says something in that very poignant moment:

> "You know… sometimes all you need is twenty seconds of insane courage. Just literally… 20 seconds of embarrassing bravery. And I promise you… something great will come of it."

Courage is being scared and acting anyway. Bravery means often fighting your own internal demons to move forward in that first 20 seconds. You just need to take the first step.

With a client of mine who was afraid to give his first business oriented speech, I suggested this concept.

"I have $1,000 to give you after you give your speech. The $1,000 comes only with one requirement – you have to complete this speech. You can vomit before you start, you can sweat profusely, you can forget what you are saying, your knees can knock, and you can mess everything up in a disastrous debacle – you just have to make it through your prepared speech and I'll still give you the $1,000. Will you do it?"

His answer was, "For $1,000? Absolutely."

My message to him was that it's not the misery or frustration – it's the benefits you'll receive from employing it.

As you embark on this new way of marketing your business, I promise you even more. If you employ the principles and practices you've discovered here – and engage the courage to be the Logo for your business – some great things will happen. Despite your own sense of fear and uncertainty, it will be worth infinitely more than $1,000.

It is my sincere hope that you will have found a solution in this book to your marketing frustration. I hope that you will now be able to stand out from the crowd and not get stuck in commodity comparisons. I believe you can emerge with enhanced visibility and a definitive reputation that provides you an unfair advantage in your marketplace. And as the clients line up to do business with you, you'll know it was because you became the kind of icon that attracted them.

If you construct such a marketing model for yourself, you'll gain the rewards in your business and in your life.

I'm cheering for you as you embark on this most excellent adventure.

"You Are The Logo!"